Managing Ministry Conflict:

Christ's Model as Presented in the Gospel of John

By Dr. Johnny Calvin Smith
Pastor
Mount Moriah
Missionary Baptist Church
Dallas, Texas

ISBN: 978-1-936497-42-3

Searchlight Press
Who are you looking for?
Publishers of thoughtful Christian books since 1994.
PO Box 554
Henderson, TX 75653-0554
214.662.5494
www.JohnCunyus.com

CONTENTS

Foreword

Touching lives with an unwavering commitment to biblical truth and teaching church leaders the central doctrines of the faith has been the passion of my beloved father, pastor and mentor for longer than I can remember. For decades pastors, preachers and laity have grown from Dr. Johnny Calvin Smith's guidance in approaching sacred text. God is to be praised for giving Dr. Smith the yearning to devote years of study to produce a practical resource for ministry leaders facing the challenges of serving God's people in this present age.

In this book titled, <u>Managing Ministry Conflict: Christ's Model as Presented in the Gospel of John</u>, Dr. Smith takes aim at applying timeless truths to current conditions leaders face in ministry. Christ did not shy away or shrink from conflict, and neither can we. By closely examining the words and works of Jesus Christ as He encountered tense moments in ministry, a blueprint for building healthy ministries while dealing with diverse personalities is discoverable. Dr. Smith has tapped into this topic in a poignant way, bringing to light the realities of and remedies for ministry conflict. Many authors have done an admirable job covering ecclesiological matters, to include conflict from a theoretical framework. Many have offered written record of their valuable, personal experiences in ministry. Dr. Smith elected to hone in on one gospel account [John] and one central figure, Jesus Christ, the excellent exemplar for Christian living and God-pleasing service. Chopped full of wholesome notes and quotes to encourage the reader, this book will be a spiritual blessing and strategic benefit to your ministry. Don't let conflict corrode your ministry. Through commitment to Christ and careful consideration of His standard for service, you too can triumph over trials.

Rev. Jonathan Calvin Smith
Family Advancement Minister
Mount Moriah Missionary Baptist Church
Dallas, Texas

INTRODUCTION

In the study of the Gospel of John, the Apostle John gives a theological presentation of Jesus Christ, who was incarnated to die for the sins of mankind. In John's disclosure of Christ, John proves unequivocally that Jesus is Deity, being fully God, and stresses the meaning of what having faith in Jesus provides; "that believing ye might have life through his name" (John 20:31 <u>Bible, King James Version</u>). Although John presents ample evidence that Jesus is indeed the Son of God, many of Jesus' own, those whom He lived among, did not receive Him; however, many others did (John 1:10-11). As John presents Christ, he focuses attention to the need for a personal response to Jesus Christ.

<u>Background</u>

Having been called a theological Gospel, John builds this book around various theological concepts, expressed in terms he uses repeatedly. John's approach is to teach by contrast – such as: life/death; light/darkness; belief/unbelief; truth/falsehood; love/hate. Other terms used are - world, word, glory, abide, witness and judgment. In Johannine theology, he presents Christ as the Word, who became flesh and dwelt among men (John 1:1-2, 14). Having evidenced that Jesus is the Son of God by calling attention to His Person, John also reveals through exposition of His

Works that He is Deity by unveiling the seven miracles that Christ wrought: Water turned to Wine (John 2:1-10); Healing the Nobleman's Son (John 4:46-54); Healing the Impotent Man (John 5:1-9); Feeding the Five Thousand (John 6:1-14); Walking on the Water (John 6:15-31); Healing the Blind Man (John 9:1-41); The Raising of Lazarus (John 11:1-44). The Deity of Jesus Christ is also seen in the Seven "I am" statements of Christ: I am the bread of life (John 6:35, 48); I am the light of the world (John 8:12; 9:5); I am the door (John 10:7, 9); I am the good Shepherd (John 10:11, 14); I am the Resurrection, and the life (John 11:25); I am the way, the truth, and the life (John 14:6); I am the true vine (John 15:1-5). Although Jesus performed these miracles and presented these claims that authenticated His Deity, John's presentation reveals that many people still rejected Jesus as God's incarnate Son.

Significance of this Study

The way in which Jesus manages conflict in His interaction with various individuals and groups, models how we should manage conflict within interdependent ministries in our local churches.

As John presents Christ's person and claims, there is conflict in the manifold responses on the part of the people. The predominate theme of this Gospel is the dual response of faith and unbelief in the person and work of Jesus Christ. Those who place their faith totally in Jesus Christ gain eternal life (John 3:16, 5:24, 6:37, 10:28-29); however, those who reject Christ are under the wrath of God (John 8:21, 24).

There are several questions that warrant answers as one reads the presentation that the Apostle John gives, mainly:

(1) What is the root cause of Jesus being rejected by so many?

(2) Why is there so much tension/opposition being built as one moves from one encounter to another? (John 5:1-12:50).

(3) Did Nicodemus truly understand what it means to be born again? (John 3:10-21; 7:50-53).

(4) Why didn't the many signs that Jesus performed before the people bring them to be committed to Him? (John 6:66-71).

(5) Did Jesus' disciples truly understand Jesus' central mission during His first coming? (John 13:12-30).

(6) Why is the resurrection so essential to the faith of believers? (John 14:19)

(7) Did the Apostle John validate his purpose for writing the Gospel of John? (John 20:31)

Although John's purpose for writing this gospel is to bring people to spiritual life through faith in the person and work of Jesus Christ, the presentation of Christ's person and work evoked conflict. I will show the reactions of various individuals listed below in the gospel of John to the person and work of Christ and how Jesus effectively manages the conflict.

Individual and Trait Exemplified	Encounter and Scriptural Reference in John	Jesus' Resolution Theological Perspective
Nathanael Skeptic	Accepting the Person of Christ. John 1:45-51	Reveals His omniscience.
Nicodemus Religionist	The need was to be born again. John 3:9-21.	Explains the way of salvation.
Samaritan Woman Traditionalist	Racial divide between Jews and Samaritans. John 4:1-26	Jesus asserts Himself as the Promised Messiah.

Jewish Authorities – The Law Antagonist	Conflict of healing on the Sabbath. John 5:16-47	Jesus asserts His equality with the Father.
Jewish Leaders - Heavenly Origin Complainer	Confused over His heavenly origin. John 6:41-58	Jesus stresses the importance of appropriating Him as the Bread of Life.
Jewish Authorities – The Scriptures Controversialist	Jesus' teaching rejected. John 7:14-29	Jesus maintains that His message is from God.
Pharisees Critic	Jesus challenged by the Pharisees. John 8:12-30	Jesus maintains that He has the testimony of the Father.
Jewish Authorities – Deity Challenger	The Jews challenge His Deity. John 10:30-42	Jesus asserts that He is God.

Martha Pragmatic	Practical way of thinking in the Divine Plan. John 11:19-44	Jesus manifests His Deity. Lazarus is raised from the dead.
Judas Iscariot Betrayer	Judas betrays Jesus with a band of soldiers John 18:1-5	Jesus surrenders to the Roman soldiers.
Pilate and The Centurions Despiser	Jesus accused of blasphemy. John 18:28- 19:16	Jesus submits to cruel treatment and the cross.
Thomas Doubter	Doubting the Resurrection of Christ. John 20:26-29	Christ gives proof of His resurrection.

Based on how Jesus deals with conflict from the various individuals and the traits they exemplify, I plan to utilize those methods of diplomacy and His steadfast drive in applying truth to every situation to demonstrate how we should minister to others by doing the following:

(1) explore in depth the individual's character as portrayed in Scripture;

(2) analyze the trait and cite the benefits and hindrances (pros and cons) of that trait in individuals; (3) reveal how Jesus dealt with the specific encounter from a theological perspective; (4) show the results of the interaction as a benefit to the individual and for the growth of the church. Lastly (5), I will make application on dealing with these traits in church ministry.

Ministering to others where there is a lack of confidence or acceptance, requires that direction be given to people to trust God in the following areas: Trust God's wisdom; Trust God's will; Trust God's Sovereign power over every situation of life.

CHAPTER 1 - NATHANAEL

The Individual

Nathanael came from Cana of Galilee (John 21:2), less than five miles from Nazareth. His name means "God has given" in Hebrew. Much is not known prior to his introduction to Jesus. He was probably a fisherman and well-versed in ancient Scripture. Nathanael was among those who witnessed the preaching of John the Baptist and had an expectancy for the coming Messiah. However, Nathanael was skeptical about accepting the Person of Jesus Christ. It was not uncommon for inhabitants to be defined by the region of their birth or travail. Alfred Edersheim provides insight as to the culture that existed during the period. "It was not merely self-conscious superiority, such as the "towns-people," as the inhabitants of Jerusalem used to be called throughout Palestine, were said to have commonly displayed towards their "country cousins" and everyone else, but offensive contempt, outspoken sometimes with almost incredible rudeness, want of delicacy and charity, but always with much pious self-assertion."[1] Since this

---

[1] Alfred Edersheim. Sketches of Jewish Social Life (Grand Rapids: Christian Classics Ethereal Library, 1904), p. 17

separation of regions was well accepted, Nathanael openly displays what he has experienced in his own town. Nathanael exhibits the trait of a skeptic.

The Trait - Skeptic

Skepticism is generally expressed in an attitude of doubt and questioning. A person that is a skeptic uses a mode of inquiry that scrutinizes and questions claims. In a negative sense, the skeptic is distrustful, disbelieving, cynical, and suspicious. In a pure sense, the skeptic may ask questions to understand a matter and will withhold judgment exemplifying a cautious, guarded approach. This type of skeptic has a sincere desire to understand the matter and is open to be convinced of its claims.[2] These characteristics are visible in the encounter with Nathanael accepting the Person of Christ.

The Encounter

In the initial calling of Jesus' disciples, Phillip accepted the call and eagerly finds his friend Nathanael and tells him "We have found him, of whom Moses in the law, and the prophets, did write, Jesus of Nazareth, the son of Joseph" (John 1:45).

----

[2]Merriam-Webster's Collegiate Thesaurus Second Edition "skeptic" (Versailles KY: Quad Graphics, 2015), p. 960

Philip's testimony to Nathanael clearly stresses that Jesus is the Promised One of whom Moses and the Prophets wrote about. However, Nathanael, who is skeptical, had a problem with the Messiah coming from the lowly region of Nazareth, and raised this question: "Can there any good thing come out of Nazareth?" (John 1:46). Offering insight on the problem of Jesus coming from Nazareth, John Philip writes: "Still it came as a shock to Nathanael to hear his friend describe this new-found Messiah as "Jesus of Nazareth" and further add the identifying description, "the Son of Joseph" (as was commonly believed). We can be sure that Jesus already had a reputation for goodness in that part of the country even though He was generally looked on as a local peasant and known as the carpenter. Probably very few people were aware of the secret of Christ's Virgin birth. Everyone, however, must have known of His remarkable reputation for honesty and integrity, for sympathy and kindness, for knowledge and wisdom, for helpfulness, and generosity, for scholarship and godliness. But the Messiah? From Nazareth? Impossible, "Can there any good thing come out of Nazareth? was Nathanael's response."[3]

Nathanael filled with skepticism failed to share in

---

[3]John Phillips, Exploring The Gospels: John (Neptune NJ: Loizeaux Bothers, Inc., 1989), pp. 46-47.

the excitement that Phillip demonstrated. This led Phillip to saying "Come and see." With the individual, Nathanael, Christ dealt with him knowing his thoughts and that he was skeptical. Jesus reveals His omniscience as He says, "Behold an Israelite indeed, in whom is no guile" (John 1:47). Nathanael being confronted with Jesus' omniscience of him responded, "whence knowest thou me?" Jesus answered and said unto him, Before that Philip called thee, when thou wast under the fig tree, I saw thee" (John 1:48).

As a man of distrust, Nathanael could not fathom the truth that any good could come from so small and inconsiderable a place as Nazareth. As a skeptic, he was truly sincere and was indeed prejudice to the idea that any good could come from such a despicable region as Nazareth. Nazareth had a horrible reputation and Nathanael would not accept the Messiah as emerging from Nazareth. As a skeptic, Nathanael needed some spiritual insight into the Person of the Messiah. In reality, Nathanael is straightforward and honest in expressing his assessment whether any good could come of Nazareth; he was not a deceitful or cunning person. Nathanael was an individual who judged or examined not by evidence, but by prejudice. Nathanael was not an individual to reason with, or speculate about the possibility that a good thing could come from

Nazareth. In dealing with Nathanael's prejudice nature, Philip did not try to reason with Nathanael, or speculate about the possibility that a good thing could come from Nazareth; but Philip asked him to go and examine for himself, to see the Lord Jesus, to hear Him speak, to lay aside his prejudice, and to judge from a fair and candid personal inquiry. Jesus, who knows the heart of all men, gives a true portrait of Nathanael's character. Nathanael really professes to be a Jew, a great descendant of the patriarch Jacob, in whom there was no hypocrisy. He was an individual who was truly candid and honest, one who lived up to who he was. He was not sinless; however, he had no disguise, no trickery, nor deceit – he was sincere, upright and honest. This was a noble testimony. Nathanael's heart was transparent and he expressed openly the testimony of his heart. He confessed what he believed without any degree of hypocrisy.

The Impact

Jesus resolves Nathanael's skepticism about Himself by revealing His omniscience of Nathanael; thus, Christ's revelation of His superior knowledge of Nathanael evoked a candid confession by Nathanael, a confession that acknowledges Christ's Deity and His Messiahship. With such an acknowledgement, Nathanael evinced a faith in Jesus Christ and would see greater proofs of Jesus Christ. Nathanael's life was truly impacted with the love of Christ and such a life can be a radiating presence in sharing God's word in a local church. Nathanael was thoroughly convinced with the Person of Christ and he became an ardent follower of Christ. As Christ dealt with Nathanael, Nathanael's eyes of understanding were open to the supreme glory of the Saviour, and he promptly confesses without any guile the Deity and Messianic person of Christ.

In the case with Nathanael, God's power will be displayed to Nathanael as J. Vernon McGee writes: "Our Lord had said to this man, 'Behold, an Israelite on whom there is no Jacob.' Now He follows up on this by referring to the incident in the life of the patriarch Jacob when, as a young man, he had run away from home. In fact, he had to leave home because his brother Esau was after him to murder him. His first night away from home was at Bethel, and there the Lord appeared to him. A ladder was let down from heaven, and on the ladder the angels were ascending and descending. The meaning for Jacob was that God had not lost contact with him. He had thought that when he left home, he had left God back there. He had a limited view of God, of course. At Bethel, he learned that God would be with him. Our Lord picks that up here and says that the ladder was Himself. You'll see now the angels of God ascending and descending upon the Son of man. The angels ministered to Him, and the angels were subject to Him. Here He was given charge over the angels. He could send them as messengers to heaven, and they would return also. So, Jesus says that Nathanael will see heaven open and the angels of God ascending and descending upon the Son of Man. He is going to see that the Father from the top of that ladder will speak of the One saying, 'This is my beloved Son, in whom I am well pleased' (Matthew 3:17). The ladder is Christ, and only by Him can you and I make contact with God. The Lord Jesus said, 'I am the way, the truth, and life: no man cometh unto the Father, but by me' (John 14:6). He is the ladder – not one that you climb, but One that you trust, One that you rest upon and believe in. That is the important thing to see here."[4] After Nathanael's wonderful encounter with the Lord, the Lord pointed him to the fact that Nathanael would see greater things.

The Application

It requires unusual patience and forbearance with an individual or individuals who are skeptical; thus, in resolving this matter, we must reason with them from God's Authoritative Word – the Bible. As we

---

[4]J. Vernon McGee, Thru the Bible with J. Vernon McGee Volume IV (Nashville: Thomas Nelson Publishers, 1983), p. 377.

encounter various conflicts with members who are skeptics, we must attempt to respond to them biblically as Tara Klena Barthel and David V. Edling write: "In a church conflict, as we remember that Christ loves His church more than we will and that He has paid more for it than we ever will, our confidence in the Bible and commitment to faithful pursuit of biblical responses to conflict will be clear and steadfast. One of the biggest mistakes people make in church conflict is failing to trust Scripture."[5]

In the case with the individual Nathanael, Christ dealt with him knowing that he possessed a skeptical nature. Through the contagious influence of one convinced disciple, many other disciples can be brought to Christ; thus, a multiplying effect of God's kingdom can happen. This is a thought we must take under consideration as we deal with skeptical people in our congregations: "They will come with their objections." We must not conclude that all questions put to us are asked in a hypocritical matter. There are some individuals we converse with who have real profound difficulties. Perhaps the skepticism is because an idea has been tried before and it didn't work. And then there's the hesitancy to try something

---

[5] Tara Klena Barthel and David V Edling, Redeeming Church Conflicts (Peabody, MA: Hendrickson Publishers Marketing, LLC., 2016), p. xvii.

new because "we've always done it that way." Even within our local churches, we should not assume we are all from the same background and thus share the same point of view. It was easy for Nathanael to be skeptical, because he came from an environment that openly made differences in people based on the town in which they were born and raised. The same type of thinking is typical in our society regarding family background, education, and professional status. We must continue to take into account the existence of skeptical attitudes for whatever reason and work to resolve the conflict that ensues in a Christ-like manner.

James Berkeley provides the following insight: "People are in various degrees of spiritual health: they differ in their ability to hear, capacity to move, and willingness to follow."[6] We must use insight into the issue and into the person under apprehension, and use biblical situations to help overcome their skepticism. We understand that we mature in Christ by studying and applying His Word. What is really needed is light from the Word, just as those who experienced encounters with Jesus Christ. In every case, we need to press the claims of Christ upon each soul we meet.

---

[6]James, D. Berkley, Leadership Handbook of Management and Administration (Grand Rapids: Baker Book, 1994), p. 177.

In his person, Nathanael was an apt illustration of one who needs God's Word sown in an honest and indifferent heart. As believers in the church begin to follow the Lord in discipleship, they will gain a greater appreciation of the power of Jesus Christ from a perspective of reading and applying the written Word.

CHAPTER 2 - NICODEMUS

The Individual

In the person of Nicodemus, the extreme religionist, was a representation of the best in Israel. He was a great teacher, a Pharisee, and a member of the Sanhedrin, the Jews Ruling Council. It is indeed apparent that Nicodemus was very religious and was very curious about the Person of Christ. Although a moral and religious man, Nicodemus was a picture of an unsaved person, being devoid of understanding spiritual things. He was scrupulous in his observance of the law, yet he was unsaved. He came to Jesus by night under the disguise of religion, yet he was in spiritual darkness. Nicodemus had an inadequate comprehension of who Jesus is, resulting in him being an example of one who had a partial understanding of the Person of Christ; yet is not born again. From the Gospel history, we know him to have been cautious by nature and educated, and timid of character, though possessing tremendous wealth. Nicodemus in his encounter with Jesus expresses the attitude of a religionist.

The Trait - Religionist

A religionist tends to exhibit excessive and exaggerated zeal toward his religious beliefs. By exhibiting steadfast beliefs, a religionist may be viewed as arrogant or prideful. The religionist has high regard for the education and training that he has amassed and tends to associate only with individuals who share the same pointed views and is often very legalistic. Nicodemus would be an example of one who possessed religious credentials, but he didn't have the spiritual capacity to comprehend the new birth experience.

The Encounter

The signs that Jesus wrought had spurred an interest in Nicodemus. He waits to have an uninterrupted meeting with Jesus. An insight as to how that meeting unfolds is presented by Alfred Edersheim. "From John 19: 27 we might infer that John had a home in Jerusalem itself – which, considering the simplicity of living at the time, and the cost of houses, would not necessarily imply that he was rich - the scene about to be described would have taken place under the roof of him who has given us its record. In any case, the circumstances of life at the time are so well known, that we have no difficulty in realizing the surroundings. It was night - one of the nights in that Easter week so full of marvels. Perhaps we may be allowed to suppose that, as so often in analogous circumstances, the spring-wind sweeping up the narrow streets of the City, had suggested the comparison, which was so full of deepest teaching of Nicodemus. Up in the simply furnished 'guest-chamber' on the roof, the lamp was still burning, and the Heavenly Guest still busy with thought and words. There was no need for Nicodemus to pass through the house, for an outside stair led to the upper room. It was night, when Jewish superstition would keep men at home; a wild, gusty spring night, when loiterers would not be in the streets; and no one would see him at that hour as he ascended the outside steps that led up to the 'guest chamber'. His errand was soon told: one sentence, that which admitted the Divine Teachership of Jesus, implied all the questions he could wish to ask. Nay, his very presence there spoke them. Or, if otherwise, the answer of Jesus spoke them."[7]

After Nicodemus' assessment of Christ as a teacher come from God and acknowledging the miracles wrought (John 3:2), Christ, the masterful Instructor, gets to the heart of Nicodemus' issue by saying "Verily, verily, I say unto thee, Except a man be born again, he cannot see the kingdom of God" (John 3:3).

But, he was a Pharisee, a ruler of the Jews, no

---

[7]Alfred Edersheim, The Life and Times of Jesus the Messiah (Grand Rapids: Wm. B. Eerdmans, 1953), p. 750.

doubt, a member of the Jewish Sanhedrin (John 3:1, 7:50-51, 19:39) and a teacher of Israel (John 3:10). Yet, having an impressive resume´ before others, Nicodemus needed to be born again. The dialogue continues as Nicodemus questions how a man can be born again when he is old. In Christ's interview with Nicodemus, Christ dealt patiently with Nicodemus, showing him of the imperative necessity of the new birth experience. Jesus will go on to discuss with Nicodemus about the necessity of His cross experience to procure salvation for all men (John 3:13-16). Christ expounds on the necessity of His death for all men by referring to an incident in Numbers 21:5-9. Moses, the servant of God, was instructed by the Lord to make a serpent of brass and fix it on a pole, and all of the disobedient people who were bitten by serpents needed only to look in faith to the brazen object and live.

The Impact

Thus, in Jesus' encounter with Nicodemus, He brought Nicodemus to a vital understanding of his need to be born again to comprehend spiritual matters and truths. Moreover, Christ also showed him how He fulfilled the Old Testament type of the serpent in the wilderness, and that as God's Son, He was sent to be the Saviour of all who would believe in Him. In Christ's interview with Nicodemus, Christ tenderly explained that Nicodemus needed a Divine operation done in him in order to be born again. The Saviour also discussed with Nicodemus the operation of the Spirit in bringing about the new birth experience as He likened it to the sovereign, but mysterious, action of the wind. Despite Christ's plain explanation of the new birth experience, Nicodemus, a master teacher, was incapable of receiving the things of God. The Divine work of the Holy Spirit is needed as John G. Mitchell said: "The Holy Spirit comes into any heart that is open to Him, and He makes that individual a new creation. He does not patch up the old nature. Thank God, the patching days are over! The Holy Spirit gives us new life based on a new relationship with the Lord. Man cannot be born of his own efforts, you had nothing to do with being born the first time. And there is nothing you can do to be born the second time. God does it all. You cannot become a Christian by trying to remove your sins."[8]

Through Nicodemus' encounter with Christ, he was brought to his need of salvation, for he was lost. This encounter with Nicodemus revealed the tremendous truth that Christ is vitally interested in the spiritual condition of each individual person He brings into the world. Through Nicodemus'

---

[8]John G. Mitchell, An Everlasting Love (Portland OR: Multnomah Press, 1982), pp. 55-56.

encounter with Christ, he became later an ardent defender of Christ as he rebuked the Pharisees for condemning Jesus without hearing Him. To further advance that Nicodemus became an ardent follower of Christ, Nicodemus helped Joseph of Arimathea bury Jesus – "And there came also Nicodemus, which at the first came to Jesus by night, and brought a mixture of myrrh and aloes, about a hundred pound weight. Then took they the body of Jesus, and wound it in linen clothes with spices, as the manner of Jews is to bury" (John 19:39-40). As with Nicodemus, those who have had a genuine encounter with Christ, whose perspective has changed about Him, will serve as a vital witness for Christ. Nicodemus came to be a true believer after his night-time interview with Christ. Such an encounter will spur them to share with enthusiasm the good news of the Gospel. Through Christ's interview with Nicodemus, Christ insisted that the new birth was an imperative necessity for Nicodemus to see the kingdom of God. In this interview, our Lord patiently explains the character of the new birth as being "born of water (the Word) and the Spirit." Thus, Christ explained that if one is to enter the Kingdom of God, he must be born again. Nicodemus, an example of a natural man, needed to be taught the way to salvation. As Christ explained to Nicodemus the imperative necessity of the New Birth, He further explained that the Son of man had to be "lifted up" to atone for the sins of mankind. The fact that Christ was lifted on a cross of shame, enduring the judgment of God because of mankind's sins is indeed an astounding act of God. Finally, Jesus went on to explain to Nicodemus that the only remedy for sin is Christ, the "One lifted up" on the cross – and through faith in Him, salvation is gained. The dramatic conversation in which Christ had with Nicodemus was life-changing and resulted in light being brought on his darkened life.

The Application

As Jesus Christ interviewed with Nicodemus, He knew very well that Nicodemus, a religious and yet unsaved man, was in dire need of salvation, for Irving L. Jensen advanced: "Now in the design of his gospel, John breaks forth with the story of one of the greatest confrontations of Jesus with an unsaved man. The man was Nicodemus, an influential leader of the Jews. The subject of the conversation was the urgency and way of salvation. Nicodemus' informant was none other than the "teacher come from God."[9]

Nicodemus serves as an example of an unsaved individual, who would need to be brought to a saving knowledge of Jesus Christ in our churches. The

---

[9]Irving L. Jensen, <u>John, A Self Study Guide</u> (Chicago: The Moody Bible Institute, 1970), p. 39.

message of the Gospel must be clearly presented, and the work of the Holy Spirit must be operative as the person is presented with the claims of Christ. Leaders of our churches must present the Gospel with clarity to the unsaved so that they may have an opportunity to accept the truth.

The problem with Nicodemus receiving spiritual things is the problem of all natural men as Ephesians 4:18 makes known – "Having the understanding darkened, being alienated from the life of God through the ignorance that is in them, because of the blindness of their heart." Because Nicodemus was blind spiritually and in the dark, he was in need of Divine illumination. Devoid of spiritual understanding, Nicodemus was honest in his questions to Jesus as Jesus explained the new birth experience. As with Nicodemus, God's word must be believed first and then He will honor one's faith by supplying more knowledge of what one has believed.

As members of the body of Christ, we must stress the grave importance of the new birth, regardless to the degree of one's education, morality or social station in life. Nicodemus serves as a picture of many people today who are faring well in life, yet they are spiritually dead. Certainly, this interview must have been confounding to Nicodemus because he was thinking on the natural and Jesus Christ was thinking on the spiritual level. As we place emphasis on church membership and service, it should be clearly communicated that works are not the means to salvation. Religious habits, devoid of biblical foundation, draw focus away from our true purpose, and can hinder spiritual growth. Our focus should not be on worship rituals and standards, but on praise to our Lord for His sacrifice for our sins. Our primary goal in ministry is salvation. Simple faith in Christ's work on the cross secures salvation. Simply stated "By grace are ye saved through faith; and that not of yourselves: it is the gift of God" (Ephesians 2:8).

CHAPTER 3 - SAMARITAN WOMAN

The Individual

The Samaritans were known as mixed-race people, who were Jews that had intermarried with the Assyrians centuries before. They were hated by the Orthodox Jews because of this cultural mixing, and because they had their own teachings of Scripture and their own temple on Mount Gerizim. The Samaritan woman was an extremely prejudice, rude, and immoral individual. Jesus revealed that he knew she had had five husbands and was now living with a man who was not her husband. It is presumed that she came to draw water at the hottest part of the day, instead of the usual morning or evening times, because she was shunned and rejected by the other women of the area for her immorality. Alfred Edersheim surmises it this way: "This Samaritaness may have chosen 'Jacob's Well,' perhaps, because she had been at work in the fields close by; or else, because her abode was nearer in that direction - for the *ancient* Sychar may have extended southward; perhaps, because, if her character was what seems implied in verse 18, the concourse of the more common women at the village-well of an evening might scarcely be a pleasant place of resort to one with her history."[10]

The Trait – Traditionalist

The traditionalist is an individual whose beliefs are centered on tradition and keeping things the way they are, favoring established ideas and conditions. Traditions are handed down from one period in time to another or from one generation to another. The traditionalist is guarded and fearful, and is hesitant to step out of the familiar comfort zone. The traditionalist supports the established customs of the society and has no desire to change them. Traditions in cultural backgrounds are guarded the most. From a negative perspective, the traditionalist is resistant to new ideas and change. Growth is stagnant and the outlook for the future holds no surprises.

The Encounter

Jesus' encounter with the woman of Samaria was no mere accident. He knew that this despicable woman would be at a well during mid-day to draw water. The fact that the Lord knew He would have a conversation with a woman in Samaria can be deduced from the opening verses: "When therefore the Lord knew how the Pharisees had heard that Jesus

---

[10]Edersheim, The Life and Times of Jesus the Messiah, op. cit., p. 768.

made and baptized more disciples than John, though Jesus Himself baptized not, but His Disciples, He left Judea, and departed again into Galilee, And He must needs go through Samaria" (John 4:1-4). At the early outset of Christ's public ministry, the Pharisees had begun to manifest their intense hatred and opposition against Christ. Christ's teaching had openly condemned their hypocritical practices. As the Lord was going from Judea into Galilee, the Lord's most direct route lay through Samaria, where He meets this Samaritan outcast at the well at mid-day. He could have travelled from Judea into Galilee by crossing the Jordan, and passing through Perea; however, the direct route lay through Samaria. Commenting on Jesus' journey to Samaria, Everett F. Harrison writes: "Opposition by the Pharisees to Jesus on the basis of His growing strength is given as the reason the Lord's decision to leave Judea in favor of Galilee, where their opposition would count for less. The decision dictated a journey through Samaria, where was the normal route when time was at all a factor. These bits of information (vss. 1-4) prepare the reader for the account of the ministry in Samaria, which is divided into the two episodes of Jesus' conversation with the woman at the well (vss. 5-26), and the contact with the men of Samaria (vss. 27-42)."[11]

Jesus will use this occasion of being weary and thirsty at the well to speak with the vile, immoral outcast woman of Samaria about the need of drinking of the living water that He offers. Diverting her attention from the hostility that existed between the Jews and the Samaritans, Christ began to express the Samaritan woman's need of salvation.

Jesus' patient conversation with this Samaritan outcast was not altogether in vain, for now we can discern that her darkened understanding was about to be illuminated. Again, her understanding of Christ as the "Water of Life" and the "Source of Eternal Life" had not yet dawned upon her; she was still so preoccupied with physical water, not knowing that she was in the presence of One who can satisfy her spiritual thirst. Having gotten her attention, and aroused her curiosity, Jesus brings to light her guilt by making a strange request – "Go call thy husband and come hither" (John 4:16). This Samaritan outcast must come to the realization that she has a desperate need that only Jesus Christ can meet and satisfy.

This poor, wretched Samaritan woman, who is an illustration of any unsaved person, is now under deep conviction and her immoral condition is candidly

---

[11]Everett F. Harrison, John The Gospel of Faith (Chicago: Moody Press, 1962), p. 29-30.

exposed, for she replied to Jesus by saying, "I have no husband" (John 4:17). Jesus Christ went on to tell this woman about her immoral lifestyle. Having brought this Samaritan outcast to a point of conviction, Jesus listens to her flimsy religious argument in her attempt to divert attention from her real spiritual need. Her real need was that she needed to receive Jesus Christ and His free gift of "living water." After acknowledging her belief in the coming Messiah, Jesus Christ makes an emphatic claim in saying, "I that speak unto thee am He" (John 4:26). Having made the definitive statement, Jesus' conversation with this once immoral and vile Samaritan woman, comes to an abrupt conclusion.

The Impact

Jesus Christ, being a Jew, brought this immoral woman face to face with Himself and showed her what kind of a life she was leading. Her loose view of marriage is not unlike the view taken today by many people. Christ did not condemn her or pass judgment upon her, but He did reveal to her that He is the only One who could meet her deepest needs. Through Christ's encounter with the Samaritan woman, He brought her to understand that He alone could satisfy the deep longings of her soul, and that He was the Prophesied Messiah. Although the Samaritan woman was quite aware of the racial, cultural, and religious differences that divided the Samaritans and the Jews, she was slow to recognize God's provision of salvation through the Person of Jesus Christ. It was apparent that racial hostility existed between the Jews and the Samaritans.

Jesus going through Samaria was a picture of Sovereign grace. It had been foreordained from all eternity that the Saviour should go through Samaria and meet the Samaritan woman, soliciting a drink. Our Lord had come to do His Father's will, and in doing so, He meets a woman devoid of spiritual life. It was no mere accident that Jesus met this woman, for the great occasion was directed by His providence. Christ met this woman at the well because He knew of her deep need. He was there to overcome her prejudices, there to subdue her rebellious will as He invites Himself to her. As Christ conversed with the outcast Samaritan woman, He presented Himself to her as the great "Living Water." He exposed the Samaritan woman for her desperate condition and need of the "Living Water." In her initial conversation with Jesus, the woman of Samaria only saw Christ as a Jew, for she was ignorant of the fact that she was conversing with the Lord of Glory. The root issue of this woman was that she didn't know of her need, nor the One who can best minister to her need. The gift of "Living Water" is all the Samaritan woman needed to bring refreshment to her parched soul. Christ, the wondrous giver of the "Living Water," won this despised Samaritan. As this woman of Samaria continued in her conversation with the Saviour, the light of her understanding began to be evident as she listened to the Authoritative voice of the Saviour. This woman of Samaria had a meeting with Jesus Christ and her life was changed – she overcame her prejudice attitude, and now we find her making a request – "Sir, give me this water, that I thirst not, neither come hither to draw" (John 4:15).

The impact of Christ's life-changing conversation with the Samaritan woman prompted her to become a vital witness to the Samaritans as Walvoord and Zuck said: "The witness of the woman led to the Samaritans' personal confrontation with Jesus. He stayed with them two days. The word "stayed" (from meno, to remain, to abide) is a favorite Johannine theological term (c.f. 3:36; 6:56; 15:4; etc.; and comments on 1:38). Because of His words many more became believers. "Words" is singular in Greek ("His word"). His message was the cause of their faith. Personal testimony plus the message of Jesus is still God's means of salvation."[12]

But, did His meeting with her produce any result?

---

[12]John F. Walvoord and Roy B. Zuck, The Bible Knowledge Commentary (Colorado Springs: David C. Cook, 1983), pp. 287-288.

Yes, His meeting with her changed her life for the better. This once despised Samaritan became a vibrant missionary, for she indeed had a life-changing meeting with the Master.

The Application

In our churches, we need to focus on the fact that the Gospel is for all people, regardless to one's social background, ethnicity or economic status. All need to be saved. All are to be reached. In Christ, sociological and other divisions are transcended. The church should witness to all men because God's love transcends racial barriers. Racial prejudice is not foreign in the world today, even among our churches. It is encouraging to know that progress on racism has been atoned for among several denominations. "Racism has infiltrated every sector in the United States – the armed forces, schools, housing and yes, even the church. After the civil rights movement, a number of religious denominations began to racially integrate. In the 21st century, several Christian sects have apologized for their role in supporting slavery, segregation and other forms of racism in the church. The Catholic Church, the Southern Baptist Convention and the United Methodist Church are just a few of the Christian denominations that have admitted to engaging in discriminatory practices and announced that they would instead strive to promote social justice."[13]   As members are added to the church, we must guard against what is referred to as "natives versus newcomers."   Newcomers may be composed of racially and socially different individuals from the present congregation. James Berkley makes the following distinction: "Natives are people who have been around church for a while. They "own" the church's history and style and vision.   They've manned the boards and the nursery, built the buildings, weathered the storms. A newcomer, on the other hand, is anyone the natives label as new. In some churches, people remain newcomers for decades."[14]   We demonstrate the example of Christ when we welcome newcomers into our congregation and minister to them as souls in need of a Saviour. Berkley sums it up this way: "The church doesn't belong to the natives, although they have historically supported it. Nor does it belong to the newcomers, who will probably change it and may eventually inherit it. The church belongs to God, and the congregation that keeps that fact in mind will handle

---

[13]Nadra Lareem Nittle, "How 4 Christian Denominations Atoned for Racism in the Church" Humanities/Issues ThoughtCo.Com (2016), p. 1.

[14]Berkley, op. cit., p. 201

native-newcomer conflicts best."[15]

---

[15]15 Ibid., p. 202

Managing Ministry Conflict, 40

CHAPTER 4 - JEWISH AUTHORITIES ON THE LAW OF THE SABBATH

The Individuals

The Jewish authorities felt that it was a crime to violate the Sabbath. Edersheim provides insight as to the posture of the Jewish authorities as it relates to the Sabbath. "Indeed, all that Jesus taught must have seemed to these Pharisees strangely un-Jewish in cast and direction, even if not in form and words. But chiefly would this be the case in regard to that on which, of all else, the Pharisees laid most stress, the observance of the Sabbath. On no other subject is Rabbinic teaching more painfully minute and more manifestly incongruous to its professed object. For, if we rightly apprehend what underlay the complicated and intolerably burdensome laws and rules of Pharisaic Sabbath-observance, it was to secure, negatively, absolute rest from all labour, and, positively, to make the Sabbath a delight."[16]This absolute rest was applied to the people, their houses, land and cattle.

The Trait – Antagonist

---

[16]16 Edersheim, The Life and Times of Jesus the Messiah, op. cit., p. 1011.

By definition, an antagonist is one that is hostile toward another or takes a position opposite another in a competition or conflict.[17] The antagonist is confrontational when events occur contrary to established authority, particularly with those viewed as adversaries. An antagonist generally responds to a person in a hostile questioning manner especially when the basic beliefs of the antagonist are being challenged or disregarded. He is known to struggle against the opposition in an effort to openly demonstrate conflict with what is being said or done. It is not the intent of the antagonist to resolve the conflict, but to promote his beliefs about the matter.

The Encounter

The backdrop of Jesus' controversy with the Jewish authorities (John 5:16-47) takes place at the pool of Bethesda, where laid a great multitude of invalid folk. These suffering victims anxiously waited for the moving of the waters at a certain season. Whoever was first in the pool after the waters were troubled was cured of his disease. Even if the waters were stirred, the state of each victim was of such that someone still needed to help them in the

---

[17]Merriam-Webster's Collegiate Thesaurus Second Edition, op.ci., "antagonist", p. 46.

pool. Through the Lord's matchless Sovereign grace, He singled out one man among this helpless and hopeless crowd to manifest His undue compassion.

Jesus Christ in Sovereign grace, the great helper of humanity, arrived at this scene of sick and despairing individuals. Among the many sick individuals, is a description of a certain man, who had an infirmity of thirty-eight years, and Christ's puzzling question to him – "Wilt thou be made whole?" (John 5:5-6). Instead of responding to this request enthusiastically, the sufferer only thought of some man to aid him in getting into the pool. The Lord greatly aided this poor sufferer and instantly restored his health simply by saying, "Rise, take up thy bed, and walk" (John 5:8). This man did as he was commanded and was made whole. This healing took place on the Sabbath that would prompt the severe criticism of the Jewish authorities. This first criticism of the Jewish authorities was the fact that the man carried his bed on the Sabbath. The Jewish authorities inquired of him as to who healed him and subsequently, they find out that it was Jesus.

Learning of the fact that Jesus perfectly healed this man, the Jewish Authorities sought to slay Jesus. Jesus Christ, being Omniscient and moving according to God's plan, knew that the invalid, who was afflicted for years, needed His Divine assistance. His healing of this invalid is a picture of His unmerited favor. Jesus' healing of the invalid should have evoked praise from the Jewish authorities; however, the reverse was true: they sought with enmity to slay Jesus. As the Jewish authorities began their accusations of Jesus, they charged Him with healing on the Sabbath and also commanding the man to take up his bed and walk on the Sabbath. Instead of responding to God, the Word, they sought to persecute Him. Unable to rejoice with the man who was afflicted for thirty-eight years and was healed completely by the authoritative command of Christ, these were filled with hatred and desired to slay the Divine Benefactor for healing the man on the Sabbath. John Phillips reports the Lord's response to these claims as follows: "The Lord advanced three witnesses to his innocence of the charge brought against him: the witness of the Father (John 5:17-32), of his forerunner (John 5:33-35), and of his fruits (John 5:36-38)."[18]

During Christ's conflict with the religious authorities, He will have a lengthy discourse affirming His absolute Deity. He identifies Himself with the Father as He states: "My Father worketh hitherto, and I work" (John 5:17). Because of His claim to equality with God, the Jewish authorities accused Him of blasphemy, a charge, according to them, was

---

[18]Phillips, op. cit., p.103

Managing Ministry Conflict, 44

punishable by nothing short of death. These Jewish authorities, who should have accepted the word (His claim) did not err in their conclusion that Jesus made Himself equal with God. Jesus went on to explain to these Jewish enemies that what He does is not self-directed, but His activity is always in accord with that of the Father. One of the astonishing proofs of Christ's Deity and equality with the Father is His power to call forth all who are in the grave. Because of Christ's judicial authority and power, He will summon all from the grave: some "unto the resurrection of life" and some "unto the resurrection of damnation" (John 5:29). These Jewish authorities could not deny that the invalid man was healed by Jesus and that an awesome deed had been wrought; however, because of their blatant unbelief, they failed to accept Christ's assertion that He had equality with God.

Jesus next uses the witness of His forerunner, John the Baptist. Phillips sets the stage by saying, "John the Baptist's impact on the nation was tremendous. Everyone had heard of him. His message was clear: "The kingdom of God is at hand! The king is coming!" Thousands of people had responded to his message and had accepted the baptism of repentance at his hands. National excitement had run high. Popular expectation of the imminent appearance of the Messiah reached a peak.

Then John announced Jesus to be that Messiah, to be the lamb of God (John 1:29), and the Son of God (John 1:34)"[19] Yet still, Jesus had another witness of His Deity, His works. As Phillips further cites, "So many and varied were the works of the Lord Jesus, exhibiting his divine power over the elements, over inanimate objects and the ordinary forces of nature, over demons and disease, even over death itself, that unbelief was wholly without excuse."[20]

The Impact

The healing of the impotent man on the Sabbath created a controversy among the religious authorities. In addition, Jesus' claim that God was His Father suggested to the Jewish authorities that Jesus was committing blasphemy. This miracle of Christ healing an impotent man on the sabbath was the beginning of the hatred and opposition to the person of Christ. This conflict grows worse from John chapters 7-12, and finally leads to the crucifixion of Christ. These religious authorities were ignorant and closed-minded to the truth that Jesus had the authority and the prerogative to do as the Father does, and that He is equal with the Father in works (John 5:17-21);

---

[19]19 Phillips, op. cit., p. 112.

[20]20 Ibid., p. 113.

Managing Ministry Conflict, 46

equal in judgment (John 5:22); equal in honor (John 5:22). Jesus had a prerogative to heal the impotent man on the sabbath, because as God, He possessed the power to heal and to give life. In Jesus Christ's controversy with them, He exposes their ignorance to the truth. In presenting the truth to the religious authorities, Christ stressed that He had unity with the Father, and had a prerogative over both life and death. By healing the impotent man on the Sabbath, Jesus was manifesting that He was God, working in unity with the Father.

Jesus really exposed the religious authorities to the fact that they did not know the scriptures; for had they known the scriptures, they would have known that the Scriptures testified about Christ. The Jews searched the Scriptures, but their blinded eyes failed to see the truth. Moses, the giver of the law, wrote of Christ and would accuse them at the judgment. Christ further exposed these religious leaders to the fact that they studied the scripture as an end, and not as a means to an end, for John Stott makes this helpful analysis: "Having considered the wrong use of Scripture, we are now ready to turn to the right use of Scripture. The next phrase in what Jesus says makes this clear: 'These are the very Scriptures that testify about me, yet you refuse to come to me to have life.' In these words the purpose of Scripture is made plain. Far from being an end in itself, Scripture is a means to the end of finding life in Christ. It therefore bears witness to Christ, so that people will come to Christ for life. Yet the Jews had missed both these points."[21]

The Application

In our churches, we will experience those individuals who will approach matters in an antagonistic manner. They will question and challenge ideas, programs, and even theology, that do not conform to their way of thinking. As we do not want this type of negativism to spread among the congregation, we will need to address the issue as Jesus did. We will need to understand the view of the antagonist and begin step by step to respond to each concern. At the same time, we have the opportunity to address the manner in which concerns are raised. It is clearly permissible to ask questions when something is not understood, but an antagonistic manner should be discouraged. We must ensure that all matters are handled in a respectful manner. Not only should respect be demonstrated in business matters, but in Bible study groups, and all auxiliary meetings. We must continue to remind ourselves and our congregation that the work being done is not for our glory but for the Glory of God. As Christ

---

[21]21 John Stott, Christ in Conflict (Downers Gove, IL: InterVarsity Press, 2013), p.89.

interacted with the Jewish authorities, He authoritatively presented the truth, and as leaders in our churches, we should remain steadfast in the presentation of the truth. It is imperative that the truth is presented because all men will be judged by Christ. Whether saved or lost, they are going to appear before Him, either at the Judgment Seat of Christ (church) or at the Great White Throne (unbelievers). The Lord Jesus gave His life for all men and that truth should be presented.

Every man is responsible for accepting or rejecting the truth. It needs to be stressed that the Lord came the first time to die for sinful mankind; however, during His Second Coming, He is coming back to judge mankind. Furthermore, it needs to be stressed that every man will hear the authoritative voice of Jesus Christ.

CHAPTER 5 - JEWISH LEADERS
ON HEAVENLY ORIGIN

The Individuals

The Jewish leaders (John 6:41-58) are murmuring because the Lord had made an explicit claim that He is the "bread which came down from Heaven." These religious leaders were greatly offended by Jesus' claim. They would not accept Christ's claim because these leaders were familiar with the fact that Joseph and Mary were His parents; in addition, the reality of them not accepting the claim of Christ was their ignorance to the superb glory of Christ. These leaders were filled with unbelief, and they failed to accept the Saviour because they didn't feel any need for Him. These leaders readily understood that Christ's claim meant that He had a Divine Origin, and their rejection of His claim only revealed their moral condition of unbelief. These leaders had no real hunger for the "Bread of Life," because of their stubborn condition of being self-righteous. Instead of acceptance, the Jewish leaders complained.

The Trait – Complainer

One who complains expresses a charge against another particularly as it relates to an established pattern of thinking or behavior. The complainer often expresses his dissatisfaction in an open forum to influence others with his beliefs. Other definitions include: "a feeling of declaration or disapproval or dissent."[22] The complainer seeks to have his opinion known and maintains his stance even when presented with the opposing parties reasoning or evidence. It is interesting to note that the complainer tends to notice the negative aspects of a situation and feels obligated to respond. This leads one to believe that contentment is not a goal of the complainer.

The Encounter

Jesus' controversy (John 6:41-58) with the Jewish leaders, who were very zealous for the Law of Moses, and considered themselves guardians of the oral traditions, erupted over their ignorance of the fact of Christ's Divine origin. This discourse was between Christ and the unbelieving Jews. These Jews, who were inhabitants of Jerusalem and Judea, were always in opposition to the person and work of Christ. At the center of this controversy was Jesus' supreme statement that He was the living bread whose origin was from Heaven: "I am the bread which came down from heaven" (John 6:41). They responded by rejecting His claim: "And they said, Is not this Jesus,

---

[22]Merriam-Webster's Collegiate Thesaurus Second Edition, op.ci., "complaint", p. 203.

the son of Joseph, whose father and mother we know? How is it then that He saith, I came down from Heaven?" (John 6:42). These religious authorities were very vocal and argumentative and did not want to accept Jesus' claim as Merrill C. Tenney expressed: "Two questions agitated the Jews: (1) the origin of Jesus; (2) the meaning of the utterance concerning the eating of His flesh. They objected to His claim to be the Bread of Life because they knew His antecedents. To them He was the son of Joseph, and they were acquainted with both His father and mother. Why should a person of such ordinary origin as His make such stupendous claims as He did?"[23] The answer from Jesus to their protest implied that they were rejecting Him due to their ignorance. As the dialogue progresses, our blessed Lord does not attempt to combat the argument of the Jews, only to direct them to the fact that Divine assistance is needed for anyone to believe on Him. No one can come to Christ unless he or she is drawn by the Father, and Christ offers one assurance: "I will raise him up at the last day" (v. 44). Jesus further gives support to the teaching of salvation by grace by citing the writing of the Prophets in an Old Testament reference (Isaiah 54:13, Jeremiah

---

[23]Merrill C. Tenney, <u>John: The Gospel of Belief</u> (Grand Rapids: Wm.B. Eerdmans Publishing Company, 1948), p. 120.

31:34) that talked about God's internal work in a person that prompted that person to believe. To know the Father, one must accept the Son. No man can claim to know the Father apart from the Son. Not only did they object to Jesus being the Bread of Life, but "The Jews therefore strove among themselves, saying, How can this man give us flesh to eat?" (St. John 6:52). John Phillips explains: "It is important to understand what the Lord means here by His "flesh." It is not His literal body…His flesh is the metaphor he uses for his human nature, the totality of His life on the side of His humanity. The giving of flesh is a reference to his sacrificial death, a death both voluntary ("I will give") and vicarious ("for the life of the world")."[24] Jesus made known to them that God must draw them in order for them to accept Him. As Jesus further interacts with these Jewish authorities, He exposed that the great stumbling-block to their faith was unbelief. They refused to acknowledge His Divine Origin. Their complaint dealt with the knowledge of His earthly parents and the fact that they knew where He grew up. They failed to accept Jesus as the Son of God in human flesh. These religious authorities were blind to the Scriptural reality of who Jesus is. As Jesus began to unfold the truth

---

[24]Phillips, op. cit., p. 133.

concerning His claims, those following Him just for physical bread walked no more.

The Impact

These religious leaders were obsessed with their religious pride and self-righteousness and did not want to acknowledge their wretched condition and be saved. They were steadfast in their complaint regarding their belief that Jesus was merely man, just as they were. They rejected the Person of Christ because they had a depraved heart. They despised and rejected the claim of Christ because their hearts were estranged from God. Because of their depraved condition, they rejected the Word (Christ); and due to their rejection of Him, they were at enmity with God. Through their murmuring of Christ's claim, they made it evident that they would never come to Christ because they refused to be drawn by the Father.

Alfred Edersheim provides the following insight: "The Personality of Christ *was* the Bread of Life: 'I am the Bread of Life.' The Manna had not been bread of life, for those who ate it had died, their carcasses had fallen in the wilderness. Not so in regard to this, the true Bread from heaven. To share in that Food was to have everlasting life, a life which the sin and death of unbelief and judgment would not cut short, as it had that of them who had eaten the Manna and died in the wilderness. It was another and a better Bread which came from heaven in Christ, and another, better, and deathless life which was connected with it: 'the Bread that I will give is My Flesh, for the life of the world. These words, so deeply significant to us, as pointing out the true meaning of all His teaching, must, indeed, have sounded most mysterious. Yet the fact that they strove about their meaning shows, that they must have had some glimmer of apprehension that they bore on His self-surrender, or, as they might view it, His martyrdom."[25]

These religious leaders did not believe what Christ told them; therefore, they were in a lost and hopeless condition. These religious leaders represented unregenerate sinners who would never respond to Christ because of the fact that they did not accept the "Divine drawing by the Father." The religious leaders needed the "Divine Drawing of God" to help them overcome their pride and self-righteousness and convict them of their perilous condition. The religious leaders' rejection of the claim of Christ really revealed their ignorance of the written Word, for the written Word manifested the "Living Word" – Christ. The miracle of accepting Christ will never happen when one rejects the written word that reveals

---

[25]Edersheim, The Life and Times of Jesus the Messiah, op. cit., p. 999.

the "Living Word."

The Application

This encounter with the Jewish leaders shows just how detrimental a complaining spirit can be to a church. Jesus took the time to present His claims thoroughly, even though He knew they would reject them. This discussion engaged both sides, with Jesus continuing to respond as they entered their complaint about each claim. Church members that are prone to find fault can impact not only the success of projects, but the worship experience. Additionally, the spread of the Gospel can be impacted. Complaining can be taken personally as it is directed toward a task that someone is trying to accomplish. Not only do we need to minister to the complainer, but we must minister to the person offended.

Our approach to resolving the conflict that a complainer creates must be steeped in the Word of God. The first response a complainer wants is that his concern is heard and acknowledged. This acknowledgement is not an agreement with the complaint, but an opportunity to open the dialogue. The dialogue may yield a simple fix to the issue, but the spirit with which the complaint was lodged must be addressed or else it will continue. We must deal with assurance of salvation and spiritual growth that salvation provides. What a blessing it would be to see those transformed complainers working in concert for the cause of Christ and His church.

CHAPTER 6 - JEWISH AUTHORITIES ON TEACHING THE SCRIPTURES

The Individuals

These Jewish authorities were controversial and refused to accept theperson of Christ, for their root issue was a spiritual one – unbelief.   Listening to Jesus, these Jewish authorities were curious as to how Jesus taught with great mastery.   They were not impressed with His claims, but with the mastery by which He taught.   They were curious in His delivery, not in the content of His delivery.   They held their education in the Rabbinical schools as the only authority.   They knew that Jesus had not attended such schools, so they questioned by what authority He made such claims.

The Trait – Controversialist

The controversial individual expresses opposing opinions to what is being presented.   In some instances, anger may erupt as the confrontation occurs.   The intent is generally not to accept the opposing opinion, but to make known in a clear manner the rejection of the stated claims.   This individual is contentious and generally prefers an audience.   The controversialist is quick to judgment without obtaining all of the facts.   Isabel Briggs

Meyers comments on judgment and perception in this manner: "In order to come to a conclusion, people use the judging attitude and have shut off perception for the time being. All the evidence is in, and anything more is irrelevant and immaterial.[26]

The Encounter

Jesus' controversial teaching in the Temple took place in the midst of that celebrated Feast of the Tabernacles (John 7:14-29). During this festive occasion, our Lord was so focused on teaching the people despite the imminent danger on His life. Our Lord's arrival signaled that He was obedient to God's word, for according to Deuteronomy 16:16, every Jewish male was required to attend these notable feasts: the Feast of Unleavened Bread (commonly called Passover), the Feast of Weeks (commonly called Pentecost), and the Feast of Ingathering (commonly call the Feast of Tabernacles).

As Jesus began to teach during the Feast of Tabernacles, the Jewish authorities were amazed at the masterful way in which He taught – having made this rather astonishing statement – "How knoweth this man letters, having never learned?" (John 7:15). In

---

[26]Isabel Briggs Myers and Peter B. Meyers, Gifts Differing (Palo Alto CA:Consulting Psychologists Press, Inc., 1980), p. 8.

essence, they were saying Jesus never attended any Rabbinic school of His time. Christ's critics were saying that He was unlettered; yet, our Lord turns the table and accuses them of disobeying the letter of the law by cultivating murderous intent in their hearts, for they desired to slay Christ. A company of Israelites in the Temple Court made a defaming remark toward Jesus saying, "Thou hast a devil" (John 7:20). However, we find the Lord still addressing the people. Despite their vile comment, the Lord persisted in proclaiming the truth. When Christ said – "I have done one work, and ye all marvel" (John 7:21), He was making reference to the incident of the paralytic man being healed on the Sabbath day.

These Jewish authorities were impressed with Christ's delivery and the manner or style by which He taught; yet, His teaching made no real impact upon their consciences. In answering the Jews, Christ exclaimed that His doctrine originated from God. His doctrine came from the One who sent Him.

During this occasion, Jewish authorities were in complete opposition to Christ as Merrill C. Tenney comments: "The opening sentence of chapter 7 reflected settled hostility. Jesus, it said, continued to walk in Galilee because the Jews (presumably Judeans) were seeking to kill Him. It was no longer a debate among them as to what should be done about Jesus, for they concluded that He must be destroyed.

From this point on to the crisis at the close of chapter 11, Jesus was living on borrowed time as far as His enemies were concerned. To them it was a matter of catching Him in some unguarded moment; to Him it was the destiny appointed by the Father."[27]

Jesus Christ, being Omniscient, and demonstrating His obedience to the Father's plan, taught in the Temple in Jerusalem despite the threat upon His life by the Jews. Christ was not intimidated by His foes because "His hour had not come" (John 7:6, 8, 30). During the midst of the Feast of Tabernacles, Jesus taught with great astonishment to the degree that the Jews marveled at it. Jesus Christ explained to the religious authorities that His doctrine (teaching) came from the One who sent Him, His message did not originate with Himself, but rather from the Father. Christ's message was genuine because it proceeded from the Father. Christ's purpose for giving the message was not to seek His own glory, but God's glory. As Jesus continued to teach during the midst of the Feast of Tabernacles, He revealed the fact that these religious authorities had murder in their hearts because He had made an invalid man whole on the Sabbath. He revealed the unrighteousness that dwelt in their hearts.

These religious leaders rejected Jesus because they

---

[27]Tenney, op.cit., p. 129.

really had enmity against the truth of God. Jesus came to reveal truth, yet they rejected Him. Although, these religious leaders were impressed with the doctrine of Christ, they still had malice in their hearts for the healing of the invalid man on the Sabbath. They were more concerned with the Sabbath day being observed than they were in an invalid being completely healed. As Jesus explained, it was totally unreasonable why these should be critical of Him because an impotent man was healed on the Sabbath. He explained to them that circumcision was administered on the Sabbath; however, because He healed on the Sabbath, they were being critical. Christ taught these leaders that works of mercy should be administered even on the Sabbath. Christ revealed that they should judge righteously, and not according to appearance.

The Impact

As a result of Jesus' teaching among the Jewish authorities, they desired to seize Him but His "hour" had not come. As Christ continued to teach among them, there was constant division among them, for they despised the person of Christ. They could not arrest Him, for again, His "hour" had not come. These leaders rejected the "Living Word" because they were blind to the Glory of Christ. They missed the miracle of receiving His doctrine because they were confused with His Person. They refused to accept that Jesus' teaching came from God, and that He had been commissioned by God. In Christ's interaction with the religious authorities, He revealed that faith is the prerequisite for understanding His person and the teaching that He advanced. Furthermore, in His interaction with the religious authorities, He advocated that His commission was to honor God, and that His ministry was not a self-exalted one. The resultant impact is stated by John Phillips. "If God was to be known, it was not to be in some pagan shrine but here, in Jerusalem, in the temple. Originally in the tabernacle and then, later, in the temple, God had manifested His presence.

The structure itself and the sacrifices and services connected with it were all designed to make God known. Yet, right there, the one place in all the world where God could be known, Jesus lifted up His voice to tell the people that they did not know Him because they did not know God. And they thought they had a monopoly on God."[28]

The Application

Creating controversy over the smallest matter polarizes a congregation. You will have those that do not support the controversialist, but will be hesitant to

---

[28]Phillips, op. cit., p. 149,

voice their stance. Silence does as much harm as the expressed controversy. We must stand-up for our beliefs and not let our silence be interpreted as agreement. There is no controversy over the truth of God's Word.

As we minister in our churches, a spirit of unity will prevail if every member would seek to glorify God rather than seek to advance themselves. Every servant of God should be zealous to guard the glory of God, and not one's own glory. Tara Klena Barthel and David V. Edling express it this way: "We are called to glorify God in our church's conflicts. Rather than thinking first of self, we are to seek first to please and honor God. If every Christian in a conflicted church would simply follow this one principle, redeeming the church's conflict would be well on its way."[29]

---

[29]Barthel and Edling, op. cit., p. 133.

Managing Ministry Conflict, 64

CHAPTER 7 - PHARISEES

The Individuals

There is a sharp conflict between the Pharisees, who were men of strong religious character and strict adherence to the Mosaic Law and Christ. John Davis provides the following perspective on the Pharisees: "Josephus, who was himself a Pharisee, describes them as not merely accepting the law of Moses, and interpreting it more skillfully than others, but adds that they had delivered to the people a great many observances by succession from the fathers which were not written in the law of Moses, these being the traditional interpretations of the elders, which our Lord pronounced to be of no binding authority."[30] They were really accusing Christ of boasting as He proclaimed to be the "Light of this world." These leaders could not believe Christ's assertion because they were judging from a human perspective.

The Trait – Critic

The critic is defined as "a person who makes or expresses a judgment on the quality of offerings in some field of endeavor; a person given to harsh

---

[30]John D. Davis, Davis Dictionary of the Bible (Grand Rapids: Baker Book House, 1973) p. 630

judgements and to finding fault."[31]   This person is also known to express an unfavorable opinion of not just ideas, but also of people.   Whereas a person providing feedback would point out good as well as bad aspects, the critic zeroes in solely on the negative. The critic also seeks to influence others to share in his opinions. The critic's desire is generally not to accept the responsibility for accomplishing a task or to accept the office being questioned.   Just as the critic criticizes others, he feels that he too, will be criticized.

The Encounter
As Christ was engaged in teaching, the Scribes and Pharisees brought a woman accused of adultery. The sin she was being charged with was punishable by stoning (Leviticus 20:10, Deuteronomy 22:22). The law stated that both the accused woman and man should die. The religious leaders of Jesus' day really knew the law, but they did not apply it right. They could really quote its contents, but they had corrupt intent in their application of it. They brought this woman before Him with the wrong motive, "This they said, tempting Him, that they might have to accuse Him. But Jesus stooped down, and with His

---

[31]Merriam-Webster's Collegiate Thesaurus Second Edition, op.ci., "critic", p. 249.

finger wrote on the ground, as though He heard them not" (John 8:6). Simply put, they interrupted the teaching process in order that they might discredit Christ before the people. They wanted Christ to render a decision that would incriminate Him, either of violating the law by exonerating her, or issuing the death penalty, thus contradicting His mission "to seek and to save that which was lost" (Luke 19:10). Displaying majestic wisdom, the Lord writes on the ground. Having brought this adulterous woman to Him, the critics of the Lord thought they had Him cornered as He wrote in silence. Only the original Lawgiver was able to render the proper verdict with regard to this woman's case. With marvelous grace, the Lord turns the very law against the woman's accusers, saying: "He that is without sin among you, let him first cast a stone at her" (John 8:7). Those that brought this woman to Jesus after hearing these words, left and went their way. Jesus does not condemn her, but tells her to "go and sin no more" (John 8:11).

Christ's confrontation with the adulteress woman will be followed by His discourse in which He exclaims: "I am the Light of the World," a claim that signifies His absolute Deity. He asserted that His witness was not false, for He had come from the Father and would return. This discourse will become the center of controversy as Robert G. Gromacki writes: "The encounter was followed by His claim to be the light of the world. Christ accused His adversaries of using faulty human judgment (8:15), of ignorance of the Father (8:19), of perishing in their sins (8:21, 24), of being worldly (8:23), of being in bondage to sin (8:34), and of being the children of the devil (8:44). They reacted by charging Christ with an illegitimate birth (8:41), by calling Him a Samaritan demoniac (8:48), and by attempting to kill Him because of alleged blasphemy.[32] In Jesus' encounter with the religious leaders, He spoke the truth plainly.

The religious leaders really didn't know the Word, as John Stott explains: "Thus the first tragedy about those Jewish contemporaries of Christ, is that they studied the Scriptures, the very Scriptures which bear witness of Christ, but failed to see the Christ to whom the Scriptures bear such constant testimony. The second tragedy is this: they should have come to Christ for life. We have seen that the Bible points to Christ. But what is the purpose of this biblical testimony to Him? It is not just that we should look at Him, but that we should go to Him in order to receive life from Him. The true function of Scripture is to testify to Christ so plainly and powerfully that first we see Him, and second, we believe in Him for

---

[32]Robert G. Gromacki, New Testament Survey (Grand Rapids: Baker Book House,1988), p. 142.

life. In this way life comes through faith, and faith comes through testimony."[33]

Because the Lord had made such a profound claim to Deity in the "I am" statement, the Pharisees are seen combating His statement or claim. In fact, their vehement rejection of His statement, evidenced that they repudiated or denied His personhood. Nevertheless, in Christ's reply to them, He maintained that His witness was true or valid, and also stated that His critics were judging according to outward appearance. These critics of Christ had formed their conclusion of Him according to the flesh, but the Lord judges according to spiritual principles.

Having stated that He judges according to spiritual principles, Christ asserts His absolute and complete oneness with the Father by saying: "I am not alone, but I and the Father that sent me" (John 8:16). Citing the Mosaic law, Christ stated that the law required the testimony of two witnesses to substantiate the truth. To validate that His witness was true or valid, Christ appealed to the witness of the Father, as well as the witness of Himself. He brings to bear the utter darkness of the hearts of His critics; thus, proves that His critics could not receive His witness because they did not know the Father. Although, the Pharisees

---

[33]Stott, op. cit., pp. 91-92.

were bitterly angry with Christ, they were powerless to implement their venomous design to kill Christ until God permitted it. Because of His critics' utter unbelief, they will never dwell with Him. In other words, to dwell with Christ, one must be righteous through faith in Christ; moreover, one can only gain righteousness through God's substitute for sin – the Lord Jesus.

The questions posed by Christ's critics further evidenced or proved that they were natural men, not able to discern spiritual things. Christ cites the reason why His critics did not understand His word nor receive His witness. The reason being, there is a vast gulf between Himself and them; they are earthly and He was from above. Continuing His discourse, Christ continued to insist that if His critics reject His witness, they will "die in their sins". The reliable testimony of Christ was true, and was in total agreement with what the Father said. It is fairly evident that Christ's critics needed to be spiritually illuminated to understand spiritual things. Christ's full vindication of Himself will be manifested at the cross, and the manifestations of His Divine glory thereafter would prove clearly that He is the Messiah. Although His critics were spiritually blind and regarded Him as an impostor, Christ knew that He met the Father's approval and would be completely vindicated. Although His critics were impressed with

His words, we have no evidence that they believed to the saving of their souls. Christ declared the genuine mark of a disciple is his continuance in His word, and genuine disciples of Christ have been spiritually set free.

The Impact

Because our Lord made such a profound statement, the Pharisees combated His statement or claim. In fact, their vehement rejection of His statement evidenced that they repudiated or denied His personhood. These religious leaders (Pharisees) were challenged by Jesus to understand that they were in stark darkness spiritually, for they did not accept His heavenly origin; thus, they were in darkness spiritually to His Deity. These leaders had formed their conclusion of Him according to the flesh, but our Lord judges according to spiritual principles. Their ignorance of Jesus validated their ignorance of God, for Jesus came to reveal the Father more perfectly to mankind. Because of their rejection of Christ, Jesus Christ revealed that the Pharisees will die eternally separated from God. Jesus had revealed to them the way to eternal security; however, because of their rejection of Him, these religious leaders were spiritually lost.

The Pharisees were totally ignorant to His heavenly origin. Christ affirmed to these Pharisees that the Father bore witness of Him; furthermore, if they had known Him, they would have known the Father. They had both the witness of the Father and the Son, yet they rejected the Son. Therefore, the Pharisees were condemned because they were condemned by the Law. Jesus, as the Light of the World, is exposing the utter depravity of their hearts. Although the Pharisees witnessed Christ's teaching, they will remain in their sin. These Pharisees rejected the Light of the World and the consequence of their rejection is they will die in their sins. The Pharisees forfeited their opportunity to respond to the Light of the World, therefore, they will remain in total spiritual darkness. For one to "die in their sins" is the horrible end of unbelief.

The Application
We will often face opposition in the form of criticism in all phases of church life. Those that are prone to criticize will tend to draw others into their way of thinking. This type of individual will require one-on-one counseling. This will allow the critic to express his views and begin the process of understanding the negative aspect of the critical behavior. Criticism should never hinder our desire to follow God's Word or His direction for the church. As we minister in our churches, we must proclaim the truth, even if our witness is rejected. Christ is the

moral illumination (light) of all men; however, He is only the spiritual light to those who believe. Christ is the hope of mankind, for He is the only source of eternal life.

CHAPTER 8 - JEWISH AUTHORITIES ON DEITY

The Individuals

The Jewish authorities steeped in Judaism held to the teaching that there is only one God and it was blasphemous to think otherwise. The Jewish authorities would be characterized as blatant unbelievers who refused to accept Christ's claim to be equal in nature and essence to the Father.

"Judaism is strictly monotheistic. The worship of multiple gods polytheism and the concept of God having multiple persons (as in the doctrine of Trinity) are equally unimaginable in Judaism. The idea of God as a duality or trinity is heretical in Judaism – it is considered akin to polytheism."[34]

The Trait – Challenger

To challenge is to demand proof of a stated fact or claim. This is brought on by disapproval or dissent and ultimately distrust. People who challenge seek to protect the known familiar standards by calling into question any attempt to deviate or persuade others to deviate from the accepted norm. The challenger does

---

[34]Wikipedia Encyclopedia,
https://en.wikipedia.org/wiki/God_in_Judaism.

not shy away from a public scene, because his aim is to have his views confirmed by others. The challenger studies the person and the claims made by the person to determine where he is most vulnerable. It is at that moment the challenger launches his attack.

The Encounter

The background of Jesus' controversy with the Jewish authorities takes place during the winter in observance of the Feast of Dedication, or commonly called today Hanukkah or Feast of Lights. As they reflected about this dedication, they recalled in the past when the temple was defiled by Antiochus Epiphanes in 168 B.C. and it was purified by Judas Maccabeus in 165 B.C. The time for this grand occasion took place in the winter during the month of December, and it also followed the commemoration of the Feast of Tabernacles which took place in October. Citing the significance of the time taking place in the winter, it was noteworthy that the window of opportunity for the Jews' acceptance of Jesus was closing.

The Jewish leaders approached Jesus with a demand of wanting to know if He is the Christ. Their question denotes their utter unbelief and hopeless condition. Jesus had wrought miracles after miracles that attested to His claim that He was indeed the

Messiah who came to save people, but the Jewish leaders remained callous in their rejection of Him. As Jesus walked on the east side of Solomon's porch, the persistent unbelieving Jewish leaders presented themselves and asked a probing question that plagued their hearts, "How long dost thou make us to doubt? If thou be the Christ, tell us plainly" (John 10:24). Although Jesus had not openly declared His Messiahship to the Jewish leaders nor to the multitudes at large, these Jewish leaders had ample proof that He was the Messiah because of His mighty works He had demonstrated.

The Jewish Nation at large should have known that Jesus is the Messiah because of one great miracle which He wrought – the healing of the blind man. The prominence of Jesus' healing blind men in the gospels is an attestation that He is the Messiah. The Lord responded to these Jewish leaders that His miracles point to the fact that He is from the Father. However, the reason for their unbelief is that they are not His sheep. The Lord goes on to say that His sheep will respond to His teaching and will follow Him. He assures them that He gives His sheep eternal life; "and they shall never perish, neither shall any man pluck them out of my hand" (John 10:28).

Both the Father and the Son are in unison in nature, perfection and glory. As a result of Christ's emphatic claim, the Jewish leaders evidence their rejection of His claim to be equal with the Father by taking up stones to stone Him. Their violent response of His dynamic claim indicated the depravity of their hearts. The Lord appeals to these leaders that during the course of His entire ministry, He met the full approval of His Father. Of course, the Jewish leaders rejected Him because of His claim to be equal with the Father – thus accusing Jesus of blasphemy. Jesus responded to these Jewish leaders by citing Psalm 82:1, 6 in reference to the fact that in certain instances men were "gods," that is, human judges and that the scripture cannot be broken. If men can be called "gods" or human judges, then the Jewish leaders could not accuse Jesus of blasphemy for calling Himself the Son of God. Thus, with the scripture, Jesus logically defended Himself.

Jesus, knowing that His discourse among the Jewish leaders was coming to an end, knew that their religious leaders would be challenging His assertion that He is the Messiah. These leaders wanted a public declaration from Jesus of His avowal that He was the Messiah. Before the multitude, Christ had not made such a declaration. The Prophets of old had announced that Christ would come and His person, life and His works all attest to the fact that Christ had arrived. However, Christ had not made any public announcement that He was the Christ.

Although the Jews did not believe Christ's word,

the miracles that He wrought served as signs that indicated His oneness with the Father. Another attempt was made to capture Jesus, but He supernaturally escaped because "His time had not yet come." Finally, the Lord removed Himself from the hostile leaders, and went across the Jordan to Perea which was one location John the Baptist ministered. In this region, Jesus' ministry was well received.

During this discourse, Christ will declare to these leaders that He is the Christ as Lawrence O. Richards writes: "Jesus again plainly tells the Jews (e. g., the leaders) that He is the Christ. When He claims oneness with the Father, the Jews attempt to stone Him, "because you, a mere man, claim to be God" (33). The Old Testament in Psalm 82:6 refers to God's people as "Elohim" (gods) because of their relationship with God the Father. Jesus asks how then the leaders can call him a "mere" man, when his own relationship with God is that of eternal Son?"[35]

The Impact

The Jewish authorities continued in their rejection of Jesus Christ because He proclaimed Himself equal with God. Jesus had wrought miracles after miracles

---

[35]Lawrence O. Richards, Richards' Complete Bible Handbook (Dallas TX: Word Publishing, 1982), pp. 553-554.

that attested to His claim that He was indeed the Messiah who came to save people, but the Jewish authorities remained callous in their rejection of Him who saves. Jesus Christ, the matchless Son of God, came down from heaven as a gift from the Father, and yet His person and works were rejected. These Jewish authorities' central issue was their blatant ignorance to Christ's nature and their denial of Christ's equality with the Father. Christ unequivocal declaration that He was of the same essence as God the Father caused the Jewish authorities to challenge His claim. Commenting on the Jewish authorities' challenges to the claims of Christ, John Phillips writes: "Jesus outright claim to be of the same essence as God provoked from the Jews their response to His challenge (John 10:31-42). We note their determination (John 10:31-39) to get rid of Him. They made two moves against Him. The first move (John 10:31-38) is in two parts. Note what they attempted (John 10:31-33). 'Then the Jews took up stone again to stone Him' (John 10:31). They had done this once before when He had announced Himself as the "I AM" (John 8:58-59). The word translated "took up" here describes something borne as a heavy weight rather than something seized. Evidently, they hauled their ammunition from the work site of the temple. This time they intended to make an end of Him. They understood His unequivocal claims to be God, the most blatant blasphemy to their minds. But they did not hurl those stones. His time was not yet come, nor must He die in that way. A restraining hand held them back. Perhaps too, the Lord's soft answer gave them pause, and the stones were dropped."[36]

The Jewish authorities had a personal disdain for Christ and they exhibited their disdain for Him by wanting to seize Him and bring Him before the Sanhedrin. Having departed from these Jewish authorities as they rejected Him, many believed on Him before His public ministry ended. The Jewish authorities missed the day of Christ's visitation; therefore, they remained in their depraved moral condition.

The Application

Through Christ's interaction with the Jewish authorities, He never wavered in His assertion that He was indeed Deity As members of the body of Christ, this doctrine is very essential to our Christian faith. The Divinity of our Lord should be greatly upheld in our churches. We are often challenged in our churches regarding our views on what the Bible says, particularly as it relates to an overwhelming acceptance in moral and political issues that are

---

[36]Phillips, op. cit., p. 203.

contrary to Scripture. The Word will be challenged as being outdated and only meant for biblical times. We must meet this challenge head on with the eternality of a God who is Sovereign and changes not.

CHAPTER 9 - MARTHA

The Individual

A view of the person of Martha is provided by Ann Spangler and Jean Syswerda as "Active and pragmatic, she seemed never at a loss for words." They also further surmise that Martha was often involved in her own activities, just doing what she thought was expected of her. "She had been raised to take care of her guests, to care for the people in her household...She seemed confused and distracted, conned into believing that her ceaseless activity would produce something of lasting importance."[37]   This same Martha became upset with her sister Mary on the occasion of one of Jesus' visits to their home. Martha as usual was busy tending to the preparation of food and ensuring the proper appearance of the house and Mary was happily sitting at the feet of Jesus. Martha requested that Jesus make Mary help her. But Jesus said unto her, "Martha, Martha, thou art careful and trouble about many things: But one thing is needful: and Mary hath chosen that good part, which shall not be taken away from her" (Luke 10:38-42). Thus, we see the pragmatic character of Martha.

---

[37]Ann Spangler and Jean E. Syswerda, Women of the Bible (Grand Rapids: Zondervan, 2007), pp. 355-358.

The Trait – Pragmatic

The pragmatic individual deals with things sensibly and according to accepted standards. The idea is that established processes and procedures will yield the expected results. The pragmatic determines that a task needs to be accomplished and approaches it in a step by step manner, with the perception that if a step is missed, the outcome cannot be guaranteed. There is little room for experimentation. The pragmatic stays busy planning the next project and never tires from "getting the work done." This is the true comfort zone that exists for this person.

The Encounter

As Christ was increasingly rejected by the Jewish authorities, His Divine Glory shines forth most beautifully in the raising of Lazarus (John 11:19-44). The Lord had wrought six miracles that displayed His Divine power, and now He displays His Divine power in a most glorious way in the raising of Lazarus.

Previously, Jesus had turned water into wine, healed the nobleman's son, restored the impotent man, multiplied loaves and fishes, walked on the sea, and gave sight to the blind; but, now He will work a miracle in raising Lazarus from the grave. This miracle is John's seventh "sign" in this wonderful Gospel. Christ had raised others in the Gospel(s) from the dead, such as: He raised Jairus' daughter, but she had just died, He raised the widow of Nain's son, but he had not been buried. But in the case of Lazarus, Christ will raise Him from his grave, for he had been dead for four days and his body had experienced corruption.

John presents to us the raising of Lazarus who was from the town of Bethany as a demonstration of Christ's love and power. Lazarus' sisters were Mary and Martha, who also resided in Bethany. Bethany was a village where the greatest public miraculous authentication of the Deity of our Lord would occur. Bethany was a town less than two miles from Jerusalem; and this same village will be the place where our Lord will unmistakably prove that He has power over the grave. Lazarus' sisters sent Jesus a notice that their brother was sick, for they were appealing to Christ's Omniscient love. In the very hour of need, these sisters carried their concern to Jesus. The sisters of Lazarus acquainted our Lord with the grave condition of their brother; the Lord in His Omniscience, is never unaware with the state of any man. As Jesus replied to these sisters, He informs them that Lazarus' condition was fully known by Him and that He had perfect knowledge of what will take place at Bethany. Jesus delays coming to Bethany for two days. The Lord will show that His delay was not a sign of His displeasure or unconcern. However, His delay will prove His love.

The Lord demonstrates that He knows the appropriate time to relieve the suffering of a loved one. The Lord went to Bethany to raise Lazarus even in view of the danger in Him going to Bethany, due to the proximity of Bethany to Jerusalem. The disciples were aware of the danger that Jesus faced in returning to Judea. However, Christ was not concerned with His own personal safety, but for the Glory of God. As Christ journeys to Bethany, He knew full well that Lazarus was dead, but Christ was only concerned that God's glory be displayed. Martha meets Jesus and she reveals the sorrowful spirit of her heart, only wishing that the Lord would have arrived before her brother died. Her sister, Mary, expresses this same sentiment – wishing that Jesus would have come to Bethany before her brother died. Martha exhibited a measure of faith in Jesus, but had limited confidence in His power. Her perspective centered on timing. Christ's delay would also strengthen the faith of these sisters; for after incurring the experience of bereavement, they would experience joy in the raising of Lazarus and the realization that the power of Christ has no limits. With Martha being obsessed with the overwhelming crisis of the scene, Jesus directed her attention to the fact of the manifestation of God's glory, even displayed at the grave site of Lazarus. Martha first questions Jesus' delay, then the resurrection at the last day, and now the fact that Lazarus has been dead for four days and now he "stinketh" (John 11:39)

Although Jesus had the power to raise Lazarus because of who He is, He was always subject and dependent on His Father.   Before Jesus raises Lazarus, He enters into the sorrows of those at the graveside of Lazarus.   Jesus exhibited tender sympathy as He wept in the face of Him giving life to Lazarus' lifeless body. He wept for the sorrow and desolation that sin had brought into the world. Before Christ raises Lazarus, He addresses the Father in a solemn matter by giving Him thanks, not taking any credit for the miracle that will be performed. By His awesome power, He commands Lazarus to rise. With a triumphant command, Christ called Lazarus from the grave; thus, He demonstrated that He had power over the grave. By calling Lazarus from the grave, Christ proved His remarkable power to raise a lifeless individual from the portal of death. This miracle of raising Lazarus was Christ's last sign in the gospel of John that authenticated His claim of being the Son of God.   At the powerful voice of Christ, the king of terror, death, must release its' prey. Walvoord and Zuck speak of this great sign at Bethany as "The climatic miracle of raising Lazarus from the dead was Jesus' public evidence of the truth of His great claim,

"I am the Resurrection and the Life."[38] This unusual miracle of raising Lazarus from the dead will prove that Jesus is the great God who imparts life, as Merrill F. Unger writes: "This is the seventh sign-miracle of John's Gospel, authenticating the Son of God as Life-giver (John 20:30-31). It was the last and greatest of Jesus' public miracles recorded by John proving His claim to be the resurrection and the life. The episode is supported by the most convincing evidence of details. Bethany was just beyond the brow of the Mount of Olives less than two miles from Jerusalem. Jesus declared Lazarus' illness was "not unto death" i.e., to result in death alone, but "for the glory of God, so that the Son of God may be glorified by means of it," through resurrection from the dead. Jesus waited till Lazarus died and had laid in the grave four days, so that He might perform a great and incontrovertible miracle. The great declarations of verses 25 and 26 will find their fulfillment in I Thessalonians 4:13-18; I Corinthians 15:22-23."[39]

The Impact
Martha, the sister of Lazarus and Mary, who was

---

[38]Walvoord and Zuck, op. cit., 312.

[39]Merrill F. Unger, Unger's Bible Handbook (Chicago: Moody Press, 1966), p. 556

a practical, active and efficient individual, had a wondrous encounter with Jesus Christ. She expressed her feeling that if Jesus had arrived earlier, her brother would not have died. As her nature is to be pragmatic, Martha thinks of everything, the delay, the future resurrection, and the decay of Lazarus' body. She had faith in Christ's power, but did not identify that Jesus could raise her brother instantly from the grave. Having wept at the grave, and at the authoritative voice of Christ, Lazarus was raised from the dead. Death, a great enemy of mankind, yielded its victim, Lazarus, at the powerful command of Christ.

Jesus' conversation with Martha profoundly strengthened her trust and resolve in Him and gave her the assurance that Christ has compassion and concern for human suffering. As Jesus engaged in conversation with Martha, He strengthened Martha's faith by teaching her about Himself. As the resurrection and the life, Christ held the ultimate solution to the problem of death. Christ definitely stressed to her that He was both sovereign over life and death.

The Application

The pragmatic way of thinking can invade our church particularly as it relates to service to others. Our approach to the visitation and comfort of the sick, confined, and bereaved members can appear as scripted and impersonal. Our personal affinity for detail and the "right way" to do things should take a back seat to asking God's guidance as we minister and allow His will to be done through us. As members of the body of Christ, we should express our concern for the various trials others may experience in life. We should always be concerned about human sufferings; moreover, we should express a belief that faith in God can help solve the pain of bereavement. In addition, we as a church should witness that faith in the power of Christ can bring relief to those experiencing the trials of life.

CHAPTER 10 - JUDAS ISCARIOT

The Individual

Scripture does not give all the details of why Judas defected. Judas' surname was Iscariot that means a man of Kerioth; thus, he was from Judea, where anti-Roman feeling was strong. It is not clear what the motive of Judas was at the time he became a disciple. Judas may have followed Jesus in the hope of political deliverance from Rome. As the disciples traveled and became more organized, Judas assumed the role of treasurer. Merrill Unger surmises that Judas, "finding himself in possession of larger sums than before, there came covetousness, unfaithfulness, and embezzlement."[40]   Some scholars advanced that Judas' hope of Jesus being the Political Messiah, who would rescue the Nation from Rome, was shattered when Jesus began to proclaim that He was going to die and rise again. Judas had been the recipient of Jesus' teachings and was well acquainted with some of His miracles. In the Upper Room, Jesus lovingly washed Judas' feet. Judas participated in the Passover Meal with Christ. In summation of the person, Judas, Merrill Unger writes: "The strongest element in the

---

[40]Merrill F. Unger, Unger's Bible Dictionary (Chicago: Moody Press, 1957), p. 615.

character of Judas was doubtless avarice, and there is no vice at once so absorbing, so unreasonable, and so degrading as the vice of avarice."[41]   Avarice is manifested in an unending desire for wealth or gain. So was the mindset of Judas. His actions will point to selfish desires that would terminate in an ending that still did not satisfy him.

The Trait – Betrayer
The behavior that Judas exemplified earned him the distinction of his name being defined as a betrayer. Synonymous with the term betrayer is traitor, informant, and deceiver. The betrayer is generally an ingrate who turns traitor to the friend he should love. The betrayer exemplifies a false show of friendship to accomplish his agenda.   There is generally a motivation for this conduct which is wealth, fame, or power and potentially a combination of all three. The betrayer strategizes on the pros of the plan, but fails to consider the inevitable cons of the plan. All of the meticulous planning will seem for a moment to be satisfying, but the ultimate reward will lead to degradation.

The Encounter
Jesus was never surprised about the treacherous

---

[41]Ibid, p. 616.

actions of Judas. He had predicted that Judas would betray Him. He knew the heart of Judas and He knew the treacherous actions of Judas. Jesus had taught Judas for three years, having chosen him as one of His twelve disciples.

In the days leading up to the betrayal, Jesus directly confronted Judas on two occasions. Mary, the one who is always seen in scripture as one who sat at Jesus' feet, offers in gratitude an expensive ointment, anointing Jesus' feet and wiping His feet with her hair. Mary displayed her act of love before His burial – six days before the Passover. Although Mary's deed was highly commendable, it was severely objected to by Judas Iscariot, who felt that the ointment could have been sold and the money from the sale of the expensive perfume should be given to aid the poor. Judas was basically guilty of concealing his covetous heart under the guise of being a benevolent champion for the welfare of the poor. Christ knew Mary's motive and praised her. "Then said Jesus, Let her alone: against the day of my burying hath she kept this. For the poor always ye have with you; but me ye have not always" (John 12:7-8).

At the Feast of the Passover as supper ends, Jesus washes and dries the feet of His disciples. He demonstrated this awesome act knowing full well that

Judas will betray Him. "For he knew who should betray him, therefore said he, Ye are not all clean" (John 13:11). "Verily, verily, I say unto you, that one of you shall betray me" (John 13:21). As the disciples began to ponder who it was that would betray Him, "Jesus answered, He it is, to whom I shall give a sop, when I have dipped it. And when he had dipped the sop, he gave it to Judas Iscariot, the son of Simon. And after the sop Satan entered into him. Then said Jesus unto him, That thou doest, do quickly" (John 13:26-27).

Our Lord was fully acquainted with all the circumstances surrounding that horrific night, for He knew that Judas would betray Him because Judas knew that the Mount of Olives was a favorite resort spot of prayer for Christ. The Lord knew that these band of men would apprehend Him. The Lord raised the question, "Whom seek ye?" He did not wait for His enemies to speak; He spoke first. His question suggested that He was ready to be offered as man's substitute for sin; thus, He was not intimidated by the circumstances of the hour. After Jesus raised the question to the band of men with Judas, these enemies answered – "Jesus of Nazareth". Jesus answered by saying – "I am He."

The majestic power of Christ's "I AM" statement overwhelmed His enemies to such an extent that they fell to the ground. His enemies did not have the power to apprehend Him nor take His life. Showing His tender concern for His disciples, Christ requested that His enemies would allow His disciples to leave. The Lord is seen here protecting His sheep, fulfilling His prayer in that He said: "While I was with them in the world, I kept them in thy name: those that thou gavest me I have kept, and none of them is lost, but the son of perdition; that the scripture might be fulfilled" (John 17:12). Having affirmed that he would die for Jesus, Peter is seen trying to protect Jesus against His enemies. In his zeal to protect Jesus, he cut off the right ear of Malchus, a servant of the high priest. Peter is rebuked by the Lord in his zeal to protect Him, for Peter did not understand God's will. It was the Father's will that Jesus would die as man's substitute for sin. He voluntarily submitted to these vicious men in being arrested to carry out the Father's Sovereign will. Thus, after six mock trials, the Saviour was led away to be crucified.

The Impact

The book of Matthew provides the account of Judas after the betrayal. Judas was overwhelmed with remorse and attempted to return the thirty pieces of silver to the chief priests and elders. However, they were unconcerned with Judas' remorse. "And he cast down the pieces of silver in the temple, and departed, and went and hanged himself" (Matthew 27:5).

Because these funds represented ill-gotten gain, they were used to buy a potter's field instead. Merrill Unger sums up the impact on Judas as follows: "The disappointment of every expectation which had first drawn him to Jesus, the intolerable rebuke of that sinless life, and, lastly, the sight of Mary's lavish sacrifice, which brought no gain to himself, increased his alienation to repugnance and hate, so that Judas became capable of the deed that has given his name an everlasting stain."[42]

<u>The Application</u>

On the subject of betrayal, we are most saddened when we are betrayed by someone close to us. Oftentimes we share our deepest thoughts and even secrets with someone, just to hear them repeated. Particularly in counseling we can not afford to share detail with others because it will ruin our witness and offend the affected party. Sometimes our public prayers share too much information. The motive for betrayal can also be for fame or fortune. This leads to struggles for position whether paid or not. Most damaging is to have someone in leadership whose motivation is for self-gratification or strictly for the salary a position pays, and not for the glory of God. We can be easily led into idolatry in worship and

---

[42]Ibid., p. 616

develop programs that are not designed for reaching the lost.

Although Judas betrayed Jesus, Jesus did share his intention with the others. Not only should we guard our own conduct, but instruct others about the damaging effect of betrayal in the church. Betrayal definitely breaks fellowship and can impact the spiritual growth of the membership. Recovery from such an act in the church will be difficult and will take much time and prayer to heal. As we look at the example of Jesus, we see that He was careful as He handled the encounter with Judas. We will have to confront the betrayer, but it should be done in love.

CHAPTER 11 - PILATE
AND THE CENTURIONS

The Individual

As noted by John Davis, Pontius Pilate was the fifth Roman procurator in Judea. In Judea, the procurator's authority was supreme. The Roman garrison stationed in the province stood at his command; all important matters came before his judgment seat; he had the power of life and death; and his sentence was executed by the centurions. John Davis provides clear insight into the character of Pilate: "Pilate was a worldling willing enough to act justly if this could be done consistently with his interest, and to avoid criminal acts provided that this could be done at small cost; but if heavy payment were needed, Pilate was not the man to give it. His secret question to himself was not, What is my duty? but, What is my interest?"[43]

The Trait – Despiser
The act of despising is showing "open dislike for someone or something considered unworthy of one's

---

[43] Davis, op. cit., pp. 643, 657.

concern or respect."[44] The despiser tends to look down on those not equal in status and holds those in contempt who might be a threat to his standing. The despiser condemns a person with no regard to the outcome to that person either emotionally or physically. Such an individual is insecure, desperate, and not trustworthy.

<u>The Encounter</u>

There were six trials that the Lord appeared before: "Annas (John 18:12- 14), Caiaphas (Matthew 26:57-68), Sanhedrin (Matthew 27:1-2), Pilate (John 18:28-38), Herod (Luke 23:6-12), Pilate (John 18:39-19:6)."[45] These trials will reveal that the Lord of glory had to endure the scorn of men; He was truly "despised and rejected of men." During these trials, they treated with disdain the Saviour of all mankind. In total submission of His Father's will, the Lord submitted to the vile treatment of men as they brought forth false witnesses. After Jesus had gone through the religious trials, where He had been mocked, He appeared before Pilate. Initially, Jesus was charged

---

[44]Merriam-Webster's Collegiate Thesaurus Second Edition, op.cit., "despisement", p. 292.

[45]Charles Caldwell Ryrie, Ryrie Study Bible (Chicago: Moody Publishers,1986), p. 1622.

before Pilate by the Jewish leaders with "perverting the nation and forbidding to give tribute to Caesar, saying that He Himself is Christ a King" (Luke 23:2).

Pilate did not want the case and wanted the Jews to shoulder this decision for Christ's death. Pilate was vacillating and he cared nothing for justice. However, he was anxious not to displease the Jews so he told them to "Judge Him according to your law." However, the Jews pressed upon Pilate the fact that legally they could not carry out the death sentence. Christ, who is Omniscient, knew that it was eternally decreed that the Gentiles would be the culprits in His death; however, the Jews were equally responsible, for they brought Him to the Gentiles.

The gruesome trials of Jesus did not take Jesus by surprise, for He knew they were coming, and that the trials were a part of God's Sovereign plan. Jesus Christ knew that He had to die a substitutionary death to atone for mankind's sins. Jesus had to encounter six trials. Pontius Pilate, a procurator of the Roman provinces of Judea, and appointed by Roman Emperor Tiberius, was a coward who was afraid to carry out justice for fear of being censured by Emperor Tiberius. Pilate vacillated in his decision to free Jesus Christ. In Pilate's interrogation of Jesus, he did not have the courage of his conviction that Jesus was innocent. In Christ's encounter with Pilate, Pilate was brought to a realization that he did not understand the charges that Jesus was being accused of. He is a picture of one who was more concerned for his position than executing justice. Despite the political maneuvering by Pilate as he surrendered to the hateful charges of the Jews, it had been ordained all along that Christ had to suffer vicariously to expiate the sins of mankind. Christ had to endure these various trials, where He was humiliated and mocked. Also, He had to be placed on a cross of shame and ignominy for six gruesome hours.

Pilate had an opportunity to use his position or power in an effort to execute justice in behalf of an innocent Jesus; however, he forfeited that opportunity to placate the angry emotions of a hateful crowd. After Pilate had interrogated the Saviour, he announced to the Jews: "I find no fault with Him." Pilate strictly found no fault with Jesus, yet Jesus should have been released. However, instead of submitting to the voice of conscience, Pilate submitted to those who were hungry for the Lord's blood. Pilate then sent Him to Herod, where He endured brutal and cruel treatment by his soldiers, followed by Herod sending Him back to Pilate. Pilate began to compromise with the Jews, only to find out that they preferred that Barabbas be released, and not Jesus.

The Impact

The fact that these Jewish authorities at Jesus' trial before Pilate rejected the Son of God only revealed the depravity of their vile and damnable hearts. Wasting no time, our Lord was led to Golgotha to be crucified. Revealing the Jewish leaders' enormous hatred of Jesus, He was crucified among vile offenders. Yet, the Jewish leaders' malice only became the means of fulfilling ancient prophecy: "He was numbered with the transgressors" (Isaiah 53:7). In an effort to display his contempt for the Jews, Pilate did not change the inscription that was placed on the cross "Jesus of Nazareth the King of the Jews."

The insulting demeanor of the soldiers in parting Christ's garments and casting lots for His coat, expressed the extreme hatred and shame that Christ endured. The impact to Pilate and the Centurions was eternal separation through their despising and rejection of Jesus Christ as the Saviour of all mankind. But, to the world this encounter will set the stage for the triumphant resurrection of Christ.

On that rugged cross, and as man's expiatory sacrifice for sin, our Lord pungently suffered and met all of the demands of God's righteousness, paying in full the penalty for sin. When the Lord knew that His work of redemption, which was conceived and initiated in eternity past, was completed, He expired in dignity, never to experience the shame and disgrace of being treated so unjustly by the vicious deeds of man. In Jesus' statement – "It is finished," He had reference to all of the ignominy and shame associated with being man's expiatory sacrifice for sin, was now complete. Moreover, His proclamation suggests that the prophecy regarding His birth, life, death, and resurrection was fulfilled. "For God so loved the world, that he gave his only begotten Son, that whosoever believeth in him should not perish, but have everlasting life" (John 3:16).

The Application

Jesus Christ continued to press His claims as He was led to Calvary's cross. Though He was despised, He never wavered from His central mission. In our churches, leaders should use their position to foster truth, and to execute justice in behalf of all. There will be biblical principles that some congregants will find offensive in the proper interpretation and application, but the Word is to be strictly preached and adhered to. "All scripture is given by inspiration of God, and is profitable for doctrine, for reproof, for correction, for instruction in righteousness: That the man of God may be perfect, thoroughly furnished unto all good works" (2 Timothy 3:16-17)

CHAPTER 12 - THOMAS

The Individual

Thomas was one who took despairing views of the present and the future. Yet he was a courageous disciple, not lacking in his loyalty and devotion to his Saviour. Thomas (John 20:26-29), one who definitely possessed a melancholy and gloomy disposition, was not with the ten disciples as they met the risen Lord during their first encounter. Thomas who always looked on the dark sides of things was probably absent as the ten disciples met the risen Lord due to his unbelief. He exclaimed his loyalty to Christ, as Jesus exhorted his disciples to go into Judea as the disciples travelled to Bethany with Christ to see about the welfare of Lazarus. Thomas, who is called "Didymus", became so loyal to Christ that when Christ died on a cross of shame, Thomas was filled with pain and he lost hope. Because of his melancholy and skeptical outlook, Thomas resisted the blessedness of the resurrection, and therefore he forfeited his opportunity to be with the ten disciples as they witnessed the risen Lord. Because of the gloom and darkness that filled his heart, Thomas was not in fellowship as the Lord appeared to them on that first Sunday.

The Trait – Doubter

The incident with Thomas doubting the resurrection of Christ was so significant that the phrase "doubting Thomas" was coined and defined as "a person who is always ready to doubt or question the truth or existence of something.[46] Such an individual is fearful and apprehensive and is unsettled until the concern is resolved. When one has doubts, he looks for solutions to settle his doubts. This can lead to false assumptions and a path that is totally contrary to the proper course of action. Continuing in this cycle, there remains an uneasiness until the matter is resolved to the doubter's satisfaction.

The Encounter

After the crucifixion of Christ, and His subsequent burial, we find Mary Magdalene's profound love being evidenced through her weeping, for she was weeping because the sepulcher was indeed empty. However, she should have been rejoicing because Christ fulfilled His precious promise of rising from the dead. In the midst of Mary's sorrow, God supplies two angels to reassure Mary's faith. The angels' presence in the sepulcher was proof positive that the Lord had risen from the grave. In the depth of

---

[46]Merriam-Webster's Collegiate Thesaurus Second Edition, op.ci., "doubting Thomas", p. 332.

Mary's sorrow, these heavenly visitants raised a question to Mary in order to stir her heart from weeping so needlessly. Mary, with her thoughts on the Saviour, now finds our Lord standing in her midst. Mary witnessed the Lord standing right there in her midst.

The triumphant Lord spoke His first words from the grave to Mary, when He said – "Woman, why weepest thou? Whom seeketh thou?" (John 20:15). In comforting love, the Saviour mends the broken heart of Mary with these soothing questions. As Jesus spoke to Mary, being overwhelmed with sorrow, Mary thought that she was speaking to a gardener, as she said – "Sir, if thou have borne Him hence, tell me where thou hast laid Him, and I will take Him away" (John 20:18). When Jesus calls Mary's name, she recognized the Saviour's voice. Jesus, instructs Mary – "Touch me not; for I am not yet ascended to my Father: but go to my brethren, and say unto them, I ascend unto my Father, and your Father; and to my God, and your God" (John 20:17).

Mary, a bearer of the resurrection news, told the disciples that she had seen the risen Lord. The risen Lord appears to His disciples on the "first day of the week" (Sunday). Although the doors were shut, it was apparent that no doors could keep the Conqueror of death from entering. In their midst, the mighty Conqueror of death issued these words of assurance –

"Peace be unto you" (John 20:19). Having assured His astonished disciples that He was in their midst, He showed them His hands and side. After the disciples saw their risen Lord, their fears turned to faith, their sorrows turned to supreme joy. This statement to His disciples, signified that they may experience sustaining peace as they commune with Him. The Lord anointed His blessed disciples with the Holy Spirit as they presented the joyous message of His resurrection. His disciples were given the authoritative power to declare and announce those whose sins are forgiven and not forgiven. Christ enjoins those disciples to proclaim forgiveness of sins in His name only. "But Thomas, one of the twelve, called Didymus, was not with them when Jesus came" (John 20:24).

As the ten disciples bore witness of seeing the risen Saviour to Thomas, Thomas did not believe their witness, for he needed evidence that Christ was risen. Thomas refused to accept the testimony of the ten disciples who witnessed the appearance of the risen Lord. He needed evidence in believing the report of the ten. Thomas was adamant in his declaration that he will not believe, unless he himself sees and touches the Lord's body. Jesus, who is Omniscient, knew of the melancholy and skeptical outlook of Thomas, appears to the disciples, Thomas included, and shows Thomas the evidence of His resurrected body.

Thomas was granted the opportunity of witnessing the risen Saviour. As He supernaturally appeared to the disciple through the doors, Thomas was benefitted with seeing the risen Saviour as He appeared unto the disciples and heard His gracious words – "Peace be unto you" (John 20:26).

This second manifestation of the Risen Saviour to His disciples especially benefitted Thomas. Thomas witnessed the sight of the Saviour's wounds, and after such an encounter, he exclaimed that Christ was truly Deity. Thomas had evidence for his wondering heart, and after the encounter of witnessing the risen Lord, Thomas worshipped. The Omniscient Lord knew about Thomas' unbelieving statements and Christ presented ample proof of His resurrection to Thomas. "Then said he to Thomas, Reach hither thy finger, and behold my hands; and reach hither thy hand, and thrust it into my side: and be not faithless, but believing" (John 20:27). The witness of Thomas to the risen Saviour prompted him to make the strongest and most conclusive testimony to the absolute Deity of the Saviour, when he said: "My Lord and my God" (John 20:28). As Thomas witnesses the "Living Word" and the One who had risen, Thomas declares one of the grand foundational truths of Christianity – the Deity of Christ. Thomas saw the risen Lord and was benefitted, but the Lord pointed out that there is a greater blessing to those who have never seen Him in the flesh – yet believe. Thomas' encounter of seeing the risen Christ was a great promotion to his faith.

The Impact

Thomas a doubting and pessimistic disciple, has an encounter with the risen Lord. This encounter transformed him from a doubter to one possessing unusual assurance in the Lord. Being a doubter, the Lord had to give him special attention. Christ appears before Thomas to show him evidence of the wounds of His crucifixion. Thomas' response to the self-revelation of Jesus has great theological importance. Thomas' response to the resurrected Christ is one of the strongest testimonies to the Deity of Christ.

The Application

Doubt can create serious conflict in our churches. The Church exists as a body of baptized believers in Christ associated by covenant in the faith and fellowship of the gospel; observing the ordinances of Christ; governed by His laws. However, individuals may have doubts concerning the Scripture, salvation, sanctification, anointing, regeneration, repentance, the trinity, and other articles of faith. We must systematically present the Word of God and resolve any doubt that will prevent the spiritual growth of the believer.

Thomas' declaration to the Deity of Christ can serve as a great witness to various church members who come in contact with cults that deny that Jesus is God. The church should stand united on the Deity of Christ, and the implication of the doctrine of the Deity of Christ to the doctrine of the Trinity. The doctrine of the Trinity is defined as: "There is one God, in three persons, distinct in personality but undividedly and unchangeably the same in essence and nature."[47]

---

[47]James P. Boyce, Abstract of Systematic Theology [1887] (Solus Christus Publishing, 2011), p. 262.

CONCLUSION

As we have examined the various encounters with Jesus and the individuals, we now turn our overall focus on the questions that warrant answers as one reads the presentation that the Apostle John gives.

(1) What is the root cause of Jesus being rejected by so many? John's gospel presentation reveals that there is intense opposition between faith and unbelief. This gospel unveils that the root cause of Jesus' rejection is unbelief.

Unbelief begins with the Nation of Israel's rejection (John 1:11) and will climax with the crucifixion of Jesus Christ (John 19:17-18). Throughout this book, the Jews will reject His claim of being the Son of God, for their rejection of Him evidences their deep-seated unbelief.

(2) Why is there so much tension/opposition being built as one moves from one encounter to another? (John 5:1-12:50). The tension builds intensely from chapter to chapter due to the fact that the religious leaders failed to accept Jesus as the "Eternal Word" that came down from Heaven. In essence, they refused to accept Jesus as the Incarnate Son of God because of their familiarity with His human parents (John 6.42). Because of their spiritual blindness to the truth that the "Eternal Word" (John 1:1) became flesh (John 1:14), they would not accept that He had

a Heavenly origin.

(3) Did Nicodemus truly understand what it means to be born again? (John 3:10-21; 7:50-53). There is abundant evidence in the gospel of John that Nicodemus emerged from spiritual darkness (John chapter 3) and became a secret follower of Christ as he became a defender of Christ in John 7:50-53, and one of the morticians for Christ in John 19:39-40. He is seen as one who helped Joseph of Arimathaea in preparing Jesus for burial. Nicodemus revealed his unashamed love for the Saviour by openly identifying with Christ as he prepares Christ for burial. These acts demonstrated that being a defender and one of the morticians, he became a believer.

(4) Why didn't the many signs that Jesus performed before the people bring them to be committed to Him? (John 6:66-71). Despite the various miracles that Jesus performed before the people, the ultimate deterrent to their commitment to Christ was due to the fact that they were not "Sovereignly drawn to Christ by the Father" (John 6:44-45, 65). They were not committed disciples of Christ because they rejected Christ's claim that He is the "Living Bread which came from Heaven" (John 6:51). His miracles were an attestation to His Deity; however, His miracles did not result in the people being drawn to Christ eternally.

(5) Did Jesus' disciples truly understand Jesus'

central mission during His first coming? (John 13:12-30). The disciples were so impressed with the authoritative preaching and teaching of Christ and His wondrous miracles, until they failed to understand that His central mission during His First Coming was to die a substitutionary death for mankind (John 13:31-32). In the Upper Room Discourse, as Christ unveiled in His teaching to them the events that would lead to His death, the disciples did not fully comprehend that Judas would betray Him (John 13:21) and that Peter would deny Him (John 13:38). The disciples were looking for a Messiah who would reign, not One who would die on a cross of shame. In essence, they wanted Christ to be a political Messiah, not One who would die on a rugged cross.

(6) Why is the resurrection so essential to the faith of believers? (John 14:19). The resurrection of Jesus Christ from the dead is a guarantee that every believer who dies physically, will be resurrected and will receive a glorified body. The resurrection of Christ from the dead assures every believer that Christ was victorious over death and the grave, and that we will see Him at the Rapture with a glorified body (I Thessalonians 4:13-18, I Corinthians 15:51-58).

(7) Did the Apostle John validate his purpose for writing the Gospel of John? (John 20:31). The Apostle John recorded seven miracles to authenticate that Jesus is the Son of God, and through belief in

Jesus Christ, men might be saved. Belief in the Person of Christ resulted in eternal life (John 3:16, 36; 5:24; 6:37; 8:12; 10:9; 11:25) In each encounter with the various individuals in the book of John, Jesus demonstrated how we should deal with those with varying character traits. Managing individuals with varying character traits require that they be directed to trust God's Wisdom (Omniscience); Trust God's Will (Word); Trust God's Sovereign Power (Miracles). As God uses different means and circumstances to bring individuals into contact with Himself, there will be only two responses: faith or unbelief. As Jesus encounters various individuals in John's gospel, these individuals are greatly puzzled as to Jesus' identity that prompted them to doubt the various miracles that He wrought. As John presented Christ's person and claims (sayings), there was conflict in the manifold responses on the part of the people. The predominate theme of this gospel is the dual response of faith and unbelief in the person and work of Jesus Christ. Those who place their faith totally in Jesus Christ gained eternal life (John 3:16, 5:24. 6:37, 10:28-29); however, those who rejected Christ were under the wrath of God (John 8:21, 24). Although John's purpose for writing this gospel was to bring people to spiritual life through faith in the person and work of Jesus Christ, the presentation of Christ's person and work evoked conflict. I have shown the various reactions of various individuals in the gospel of John to the person and work of Christ and how Jesus sought to effectively manage the conflict. Ministering to others where there is a lack of confidence or acceptance, requires that direction be given to people to trust God in the following areas: Trust God's wisdom; Trust God's will; Trust God's Sovereign power over every situation of life.

Utilizing the various ways in which Jesus managed conflict in this gospel will dispel misunderstandings, misconceptions, and misalignment that can be prevalent among God's people. In my opinion, the ways that Jesus managed conflict as He confronted the various people in this gospel can promote harmony rather than create strife and division. Such a topic, if discussed and implemented, can promote concord between ministries of our churches. James Berkley concisely states: "Conflict is inevitable, and leaders strengthen their teams when they accept it as such. Conflict is either resolved (spreading grace) or buried over (feeding bitterness)."[48]

Conflict will erupt at some time in the majority of our congregations. Often this is seen more in smaller congregations because the information flows freely. When we look at the heart of most issues, we see that

---

[48]Berkley, op. cit., p. 184

conflict occurs over values, whether they are related to spiritual or social issues. In reviewing the work of Speed Leas in the book Conflict Management in Congregations there is much discussion on the personal aspect of conflict. When we let a disagreement fester, it later manifests itself in conflict. There are signs that this is happening: first, the disagreement will focus on the problem; second, next the focus is on self-protection; third, the focus is on winning; fourth, the focus is on revenge or getting rid of someone; fifth, the person creating the conflict begins to feel that is God ordained. We must avoid this cycle of behavior and seek to resolve conflict as they occur.

The resulting behavior is unproductive in resolving conflict, which leads to dropouts. Some people stop attending worship services, auxiliary meetings, stop contributing and ultimately transfer their membership. If the party cannot conform to the church's direction, this is inevitable. The church must have established boundaries and we must ensure these boundaries are based on the Word of God. Another non-productive behavior is assigning blame, the desire to point to the sole individual or group that started the whole matter. Both sides see themselves as trying to resolve the issue, but both parties refuse to cooperate. Then we spiral downwardly to attack. This involves character assassination and may present itself in subtle dropped hints, implied personality disorders, petitions, and secret meetings. We also use generalizations and tend to see the problem as huge and difficult. We move quickly from the specific to the general and tend to determine a much broader reason for a person's behavior. Lastly, we state our version of the truth or use distorted communication. Anonymous communication should not be allowed nor presented as factual.

As we look at what behavior or attitudes are helpful in managing conflict, we should keep in mind the love that Jesus showed even for His enemies and more importantly, He did not compromise His claims. We can look to be inclusive in reaching acceptable solutions and a sincere desire to implement the solutions. We should steer the congregants into cooperation and not competition. Differences and statements of the opposition should be acknowledged and heard, stressing they must be presented in a Christ-like respectful manner.

Ultimately, the goal in resolving conflict is to have clear direction without damaging relationships. We learn to appreciate differences, for sometimes opposing opinions bring needed solutions to the surface. We must realize that some people are fragile and insecure, and we are not all at the same point in our Christian growth. We should be tolerant and patient in order to help the group grow stronger. We cannot afford to lose focus on our purpose to glorify God. The church should represent and demonstrate the teachings of Christ, not just in the worship services but in all aspects of its existence. This applies to educational programs, recreational programs and outreach ministry. We cannot afford to allow Satan to interrupt God's program.

Speed Leas makes this assessment of conflict: "Actually, there is nothing intrinsically bad about conflict. It is a fact of life, and often an important ingredient in making possible new ideas, new ways of doing things, and new or renewed relationships."[49]

Christ exhibited unusual love and patience with those who basically didn't understand His person and the various miracles in which He wrought. Christ modeled that in dealing with people you must have patience and never forget that you are called upon to serve, and not to be served. And in managing conflict, Christ exhibited love for those He served. Christ certainly revealed that in conflict resolution, you must place the interest of others before your own interest. Thus, in placing the interest of others before His own, Christ modeled in His teaching two central emphases of His First Coming - "For even the Son of

---

[49]David B. Lott, Editor. Speed B. Leas, Essay, Conflict Management in Congregations (Virginia:Alban Institute, 2001), p. 10.

man came not to be ministered unto, but to minister, and to give His life a ransom for many" (Mark 10:45), and "For the Son of Man is come to seek and to save that which was lost" (Luke 19:10).

Bibliography

Barthel, Tara Klena, and Edling, David V. Redeeming Church Conflicts. Peabody, Massachusetts: Hendrickson Publishers Marketing, LLC, 2012.

Berkley, James, D. Leadership Handbook of Management and Administration. Grand Rapids: Baker Book House, 1994.

Boyce, James P. Abstract of Systematic Theology. 1887. Solus Christus, 2011.

Davis, John D. Davis Dictionary of the Bible. Grand Rapids: Baker Book House, 1973.

Edersheim, Alfred. Sketches of Jewish Social Life. Grand Rapids: Christian Classics Ethereal Library, 1904.

Edersheim, Alfred. The Life and Times of Jesus the Messiah. Grand Rapids: Wm. B. Eerdmans, 1953.

Gromacki, Robert G. New Testament Survey. Grand Rapids, Michigan: Baker Book House, 1988.

Harrison, Everett F. John - The Gospel of Faith. Chicago: Moody Press, 1962.

Jenson, Irving L. John, A Self Study Guide. Chicago:
Moody Press, 1970.

Lott, David B. Editor, Leas, Speed B.,Essay. Conflict
Management in Congregations. Virginia: The Alban
Institute, 2001.

McGee, J. Vernon. Thru The Bible with J. Vernon
McGee. Nashville: Thomas Nelson Publishers, 1983.

Merriam-Webster's Collegiate Thesaurus Second
Edition. Versailles KY: Quad Graphics, 2015.

Mitchell, John G. An Everlasting Love. Portland OR:
Multnomah Press, 1982..

Myers, Isabel Briggs. and Meyers, Peter B. Gifts
Differing. Palo Alto CA: Consulting Psychologists
Press, Inc., 1980.

Nittle, Nadra Lareem. "How 4 Christian
Denominations Atoned for Racism in the Church"
Humanities/Issues ThoughtCo.Com, 2016.

Phillips, John. Exploring The Gospels - John.
Neptune, New Jersey: Loizeaux Brothers, 1989.
Richards, Lawrence O. Richards' Complete Bible
Handbook. Dallas TX: Word Publishing, 1982.

Ryrie, Charles Caldwell. Ryrie Study Bible. Chicago: Moody Publishers,1986..

Spangler, Ann and Syswerda, Jean E. Women of the Bible. Grand Rapids: Zondervan, 2007.

Stott, John. Christ in Conflict. Downers Grove, IL: InterVarsity Press, 2013.

Tenney, Merrill C. John: The Gospel of Belief. Grand Rapids, Michigan: William B. Eerdmans Publishing Company, 1948.

Unger, Merrill F. Unger's Bible Handbook. Chicago: Moody Press, 1966.

Unger, Merrill F. Unger's Bible Dictionary. Chicago: Moody Press, 1957.

Walvoord, John F., and Zuck, Roy B. The Bible Knowledge Commentary. Colorado Springs: David C. Cook, 1983.

Wikipedia Encyclopedia
https://en.wikipedia.org/wiki/God_in_Judaism.

About the Author:
PASTOR JOHNNY CALVIN SMITH

"Being confident of this very thing, that he which hath begun a good work in you will perform it until the day of Jesus Christ." Philippians 1:6

The Reverend Johnny Calvin Smith has a powerful message for all mankind. This man of God speaks without reservation, proclaiming the gospel of grace, calling for repentance, faith, and hope in our Lord Jesus Christ. Rev. Smith is in his eleventh year as Pastor of the Mount Moriah Missionary Baptist Church, Dallas, Texas.

Ordained as a Minister at Mount Moriah in 1977, he began in 1982 serving as Director of the Board of Christian Education until accepting the pastorate in 2007. Additionally, he has served as a Sunday School Teacher, Instructor of Evangelical Training Association; and Mount Moriah Disciple Institute. He has also served as a part-time Instructor at Southern Bible Institute since 1985. He rightly divides the Word in his inspirational column, "Devotional Thought from the Word" published in The Dallas Post Tribune.

Pastor Smith has a great love and devotion for his family and a sincere passion and concern for the youth of today. He is a retired Mathematics/Science Teacher from the Dallas Public Schools. Pastor Smith expresses "I am praying that youth of today will remain steadfast in their walk with the Lord and avoid the pitfalls of seemingly worldly pleasures presented by Satan."

Personal Data
Marital Status – Married 45 years - wife, Violet Reed Smith;
Children - Daughter, Joy (Brad) McBeth; Sons, Rev. Jonathan (Christina) Smith and Rev. Jared R. (Erica) Smith
Grandchildren – Josiah, Jeremiah, Jedidiah, Jillian,

Jessica, Jackson, Jordan

Educational Background
High School Diploma
L.G. Pinkston High School, Dallas, TX, May 1970.

Undergraduate Degree
Jarvis Christian College, Hawkins, TX, August 1970 – May 1972
Southern Methodist University, Dallas, TX, August 1972-May 1974
Bachelor of Business Administration

Biblical Studies
Southern Bible Institute, Dallas, TX, August 1975 – May 1980
Diploma in Preliminary Bible Program

Dallas Bible College, Dallas, TX, August 1982 – May 1984

Graduate Degrees
Dallas Theological Seminary, Dallas, TX, August 1984 – May 1991
Master of Arts in Biblical Studies

Northwestern Theological Seminary, New Port Richey, FL, January 2015 – July 2017

Doctor of Theology in Biblical Studies

Southern Bible Institute and College, Dallas, TX, May 2018
Honorary Doctor of Humane Letters

Certification
Texas Teacher Certificate – Elementary Grades (PK-6) July 1996

Other Experience/Affiliations
Columnist – The Dallas Post Tribune, Dallas, Texas, September 1992 - present
Instructor – Southern Bible Institute and College, September 1985 – 2019

**The Baptist General Convention of Texas
Southern Baptist of Texas Convention
Dallas Baptist Association
The Baptist Ministers' Union of Dallas and Vicinity
Oak Cliff Baptist Ministers' Union
South Dallas Faith Coalition**

Professional Background
Oct 1992 – May 2011
Dallas Public Schools
Mathematics/Science Teacher

Jan 1975 - Sep 1992
Mobil Pipe Line Company, Dallas Texas
Accountant, Property Section – Performed fixed
assets accounting duties; handled cash sales, trade-ins,
retirements and transfers; maintained subsidiary
ledgers. Provided timely and accurate accounting data
for assigned pipe line companies.

Jun 1972 - Apr 1974
Channel 13, Dallas, Texas
Assistant Accountant.

The Smith Family

Also by the Author

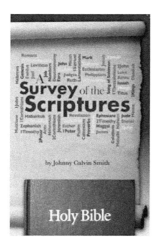

A Survey of the Scriptures
by Dr Johnny Calvin Smith
Searchlight Press (2013)
ISBN-13 : 978-1936497201

In A Survey of the Scriptures, evangelical pastor and teacher Johnny Calvin Smith writes a straightforward overview of the Bible, suitable for clergy, laity, and students. "Pastor Smith has written a book that will help those interested in Bible study to go deeper in their understanding.

CPSIA information can be obtained
at www.ICGtesting.com
Printed in the USA
BVHW010853291220
596587BV00016B/136